Pearson Edexcel GCSE (9–1)
English Language 2.0
Student Workbook

Julie Hughes

Contents

How to use this book   4

Reading

AO1
Question style   5
Identifying explicit information   6
Identifying implicit information   7
Top tips and practice   8
Synthesis   9
Using evidence   10
Top tips and practice   11

AO2
Using inference   12
Word classes   13
Techniques   14
Beginnings and endings   15
Sentences and punctuation   16
Techniques and rhetorical devices   17
Paper 1 language question   18
Paper 2 language question   19
Paper 2 language and structure question   20
Paper 1 practice   21
Paper 2 practice   22
Top tips and practice   23

AO3
Question style   24
Identifying perspectives   25
Identifying ideas   26
Comparing ideas and perspectives   27
Comparing the writers' language   28
Comparing the writers' structure   29
Comparison question practice   30
Top tips and practice   31

AO4
Question style   32
Evaluation   33
Finding relevant ideas   34
Explaining relevant ideas   35
Making a judgement   36
Short extract practice   37
Whole text (part 1)   38
Whole text (part 2)   39
Whole text practice   40
Top tips and practice   41

Transactional writing

AO5
Plan Unlock the question   42
Plan Gathering ideas   43
Plan Using the question (part 1)   44
Plan Using the question (part 2)   45
Plan Top tips and practice   46
Structure Overall structure   47
Structure Ordering your ideas   48
Structure Openings   49
Structure Endings   50
Structure Top tips and practice   51
Development Adding details   52
Development Topic sentences   53
Development Building up your ideas   54
Development Signposting   55
Development Top tips and practice   56
Style Text types   57
Style Tone   58
Style Rhetorical devices for emphasis   59
Style Rhetorical devices for impact   60
Style Top tips and practice   61

AO6
Synonyms   62
Vocabulary   63
Sentence openings   64
Sentence style and punctuation   65
Top tips and practice   66

Imaginative writing

AO5

Plan	Selecting a question	67
Plan	Gathering ideas	68
Plan	Using an image	69
Plan	Three-part story plan	70
Plan	Top tips and practice	71
Structure	Structuring for effect	72
Structure	Flashback	73
Structure	Openings	74
Structure	Endings	75
Structure	Top tips and practice	76
Development	Adding details to your plan	77
Development	Character creation	78
Development	Settings	79
Development	Paragraphs	80
Development	Top tips and practice	81
Style	Tone	82
Style	Metaphors and similes	83
Style	Figurative language	84
Style	Using the senses	85
Style	Top tips and practice	86

AO6

Vocabulary	87
Imagery	88
Sentence openings	89
Sentence style and punctuation	90
Proof reading	91
Top tips and practice	92

Reading texts

Text A	19th c. Bathing in the River	93
Text B	19th c. Baths by the Sea	94
Text C	19th c. Memories of London	95
Text D	19th c. Flowing Hair for Ladies	96
Text E	19th c. The Moustache	97
Text F	19th c. Manners	98
Text G	20th c. Saturday Night and Sunday Morning	99
Text H	21st c. Teacher Man	100
Text I	20th c. Once in a House on Fire	101
Text J	21st c. The Hate U Give	102
Text K	21st c. Clothes, clothes, clothes, music, music, music, boys, boys, boys	103
Text L	20th c. About a Boy	104

How to use this book

This book helps you develop and improve the skills you need for the English Language 2.0 GCSE course. The book has three sections – Reading, Transactional writing, and Imaginative writing. Each section is broken down into the following key skills. All these skills are assessed in the two exams that you will take for this qualification.

Reading

AO1
Identify and interpret explicit and implicit information and ideas.
Select and synthesise evidence from different texts.

AO2
Analyse how writers use language and structure to achieve effects and influence readers, using relevant subject terminology to support their views.

AO3
Compare writers' ideas and perspectives, as well as how these are conveyed, across two or more texts.

AO4
Evaluate texts critically and support this with appropriate textual references.

Writing

AO5
Communicate clearly, effectively and imaginatively, selecting and adapting tone, style and register for different forms, purposes and audience.
Organise information and ideas using structural and grammatical features to support coherence and cohesion of texts.

AO6
Use a range of vocabulary and sentence structures for clarity, purpose and effect, with accurate spelling and punctuation.

You can work through the skills in whichever order you choose. There is an introduction to each skill, step-by-step guidance on how to approach and answer each type of question, and extracts from example answers. Each page has a '**have a go**' task to help build your confidence as you work towards answering exam-style questions. **Top Tips** provide pointers on what the examiners are looking for and advice on how to avoid common pitfalls.

Extracts for reading tasks are included on the page or at the back of the book. Each extract has audio which can be accessed by scanning the QR code next to it.

Text extract

> Colin and Raymond scowl up at him; they are not happy to be here or grateful for their second chance.

Sample student answer

> The writer says that 'the ride' is 'not a long one' which suggests that trains are fast and speedy.

Top tips

Top tips:

- Find ideas or opinions in the text that are relevant to the question.

Now have a go

Now **have a go**. Look at text D 'Flowing Hair for Ladies' on page 96.

Question 1. Highlight at least two words, phrases or techniques you think are interesting or informative and use inference to explain their effect.

AO1

Identify and interpret explicit and implicit information and ideas. Select and synthesise evidence from different text.

Question style

AO1 is in two parts. The first will assess your ability to find and interpret information in a text. The second will ask you to synthesise two texts and identify similarities.

For instance:

> Identify ❶four pieces of ❷advice the writer gives about swimming.

❶ The number of answers needed is clearly shown.

❷ This question is asking for explicit information, so a short quotation is all that is needed.

> From this extract, identify ❶one way the ❸writer shows he wants to be saved.

❸ This question is asking for implicit information, so inference ('reading between the lines') is needed.

Remember: Answers for both question types could be short quotations or a paraphrase (putting the answer in your own words).

> Text 1 and text 2 both show people living in high rise buildings. The buildings are different, but they share similarities.
>
> ❹Write a summary giving three different ways the experiences of living in high buildings are similar.
>
> ❺Support each similarity with evidence from both texts.

❹ Three brief summary sentences are needed.

❺ Use short quotations or paraphrases to support the summary sentences.

Now **have a go.** Decide if the following statements are **True** or **False**. Circle the correct answers.

- You must answer AO1 questions in full sentences. **True / False**
- Lengthy quotations must be used support summary sentences. **True / False**
- You can use paraphrasing as evidence. **True / False**

AOI — Identifying explicit information

Identifying explicit information means you need to find something that is clearly stated in the text. You do not need to explain your answer – just find a short quotation or paraphrase (put the answer into your own words).

For instance, look at this question which is asking for explicit information from a **19th** century text about travelling by train. The student's answers are short quotations and do not use full sentences. Two of them are correct, but one is incorrect as it is not something that is seen from the train.

Identify four things the narrator sees from the train.

> Other trains pass by, but you can't see them. There's a sudden stop at a station, with the thousand faces of the waiting crowd lit up as if by a great fire; and then off we go again, with a deafening noise of doors being slammed shut, bells being rung, machinery grunting; again darkness, more trains passing by, more glimpses of daylight, more illuminated stations, more crowds of people passing, arriving, leaving, until we reach the terminus.

The waiting crowd ✓

Trains passing by ✓

Doors being slammed ✗

Now **have a go.**

Identify two more things the narrator sees from the train.

- _____
- _____

Identifying implicit information

AOI

Identifying implicit information in a text means interpreting what a writer is suggesting or implying. This is sometimes called 'reading between the lines', or using inference. You can answer these question types with a short quotation, a short paraphrase, or a mixture of both.

For instance, look at this question about a text where a narrator is describing a maths lesson.

From the extract, identify one way that the narrator shows they are excited by their knowledge.

> Next lesson, I couldn't resist.
>
> 'Five *x* plus three *y*, Sir.'
>
> Up shot my hand, out flew the words. No hisses from the back row.
>
> 'Seven *x* minus two *y*.'
>
> Once could be passed off as an accident. Twice was something else.

They 'couldn't resist' answering the question.

Now **have a go.** Questions like the one above will always have more than one possible answer.

Read the short extract again and find two more ways the narrator shows she is excited by her knowledge.

- _____
  _____
- _____
  _____

AO1 — Top tips and practice

Top tips:

- Read the extract carefully before starting to answer the question.
- If the question gives line numbers, or has a short extract, use only that part of the text to find your answer.
- If no lines numbers are given, look at the whole of the text to find your answers.
- Use short quotations or paraphrase, **not** full sentences.
- **Watch the time!** These questions are one mark only per answer, so do not spend too long on them.

Have a go at the following AO1 questions.

> Read text B 'Baths by the Sea' on page **94**.
>
> From lines **25** to **30**, identify **two** pieces of advice the writer gives about spending time on the beach.

1. _____
2. _____

Read this extract:

> Take plenty of exercise, but do not fatigue yourself, and beware of a too hot sun. Go to bed early and be up before the mists of morning have quite gathered themselves off the sea. Do not forget that the evenings are often chilly; it is well, therefore, if you mean to enjoy a walk after nightfall, to change your dress for it, putting on thicker boots, and flannels ought always to be worn, for the changes of temperature are often very trying even to the robust.

From this extract, identify **two** ways the writer suggests that exercising is challenging.

1. _____
2. _____

Synthesis

AOI

On Paper 2, you need to synthesise information from the two texts. This means looking at the two texts together and finding things that they have in common, such as similarities between the people, places or events described. You then need to write brief sentences summarising the similarities you have found.

For instance, look at two similarities which have been briefly summarised from two texts about teenage friendship.

❶ Both have invitations to visit friend's houses.

I made the mistake of ❶inviting them to a sleepover in seventh grade. Momma was gonna let us do our nails, stay up all night and ❷eat as much pizza as we wanted.

Tamsyn's mother and father had ❶invited me to their house in Didsbury for ❷tea, which they called dinner.

❷ Both involve eating a meal.

Now **have a go**. Read the question below and then read text I 'Once in a House on Fire' on page **101** and text J 'The Hate U Give' on page **102**. Find and summarise two more similarities between the texts.

> Text I and text J both describe experiences of teenage friendship. The experiences are different, but they share similarities.
>
> Write a summary giving **two** different ways the experiences of the teenagers are similar.

Both _____

_____

Both _____

_____

AOI Using evidence

When answering a synthesis question, you need to use clear, appropriate evidence from each text to support your similarities. You do not need to explain your evidence, it just needs to relate clearly to the similarity you have found.

For instance, look at this synthesis question. Then look at the start of a student response – they have used evidence to support one similarity between the two texts.

> Text 1 and text 2 both describe experiences of teenage friendship. The experiences are different, but they share similarities.
>
> Write a summary giving three different ways the experiences of the teenagers are similar.
>
> Support each similarity with evidence from both texts.

Both involve invitations to visit friend's houses.

In text 1, Thomas says ❶'inviting them to a sleepover'.

In text 2, Ashworth says ❶'Tamsyn's mother and father had invited me to their house'.

❶ Use a short supporting quotation from each text, with each text clearly identified by the text number or the writer's name. No explanation or inference is needed.

Now **have a go**. Read the question again. Then read text I 'Once in a House on Fire' on page **101** and text J 'The Hate U Give' on page **102**. Now complete the student's answer below.

> Both write about eating a meal.
>
> In text I, Thomas says _____
>
> In text J, Ashworth says _____
>
> Both _____
>
> In text I, Thomas says _____
>
> In text J, Ashworth says _____

Top tips and practice

AO1

Top tips:

- Look at the whole of both extracts to find similarities.
- Focus on similarities between concrete things such as people, events or places. **Do not** write about language or structure similarities.
- Start your summary sentences with 'Both' and keep them brief.
- Use evidence from **each** text.
- Make it clear which text your evidence is from by referring to the texts as, for example, 'text 1' or by using the writer's surname.

Now **have a go** at the following AO1 synthesis question. Read the extracts carefully first.

Read text G 'Saturday Night and Sunday Morning' on page **99** and text H 'Teacher Man' on page **100**. Remember this would only be worth **6** marks in the exam, so be concise.

> Text G and text H both show people at work. The experiences are different, but they share similarities.
>
> Write a summary giving **three** different ways the experiences of work are similar.
>
> Support each similarity with evidence from both texts.

Both _____
_____
_____

Both _____
_____
_____

Both _____
_____
_____

11

AO2

Analyse the language, form and structure used by a writer to create meanings and effects, using relevant subject terminology where appropriate.

Using inference

AO2 language questions ask you to consider the effect of a writer's choices. To do this, you need to use **inference** to consider the **connotations** of words and phrases. Think about what the words or phrases mean within the text – don't just think about literal meanings.

For instance, look at this extract where a writer is describing his parents.

> Dad appeared first. Slouched and barefoot, he walked up to me slowly, ❶shook my hand, ❷patted me on the back and returned soundlessly to his armchair in the living room. Next, Mum came out of the kitchen ❸smiling, looking broad in a chunni, a scarf and a shawl, and gave me a suffocating hug.

❶ Very formal greeting suggests father not very good at showing emotion.

❷ 'Patted' is a way adults greet children, suggests father still sees his son as a child.

❸ Suggests happiness at seeing son.

Now **have a go** at using inference on some other words and phrases in the extract.

Question 1. How does the phrase 'slouched and barefoot' suggest that the father may be unwell?

_____
_____
_____
_____

Question 2. How does the phrase 'suffocating hug' suggest that his mother still treats the narrator as a child?

_____
_____
_____
_____

Word classes

AO2

When looking at a writer's language choices, you need to consider the effect of different word classes, such as verbs, adjectives and nouns.

For instance, look at the effect of the writer's choice of words in this extract about going into the London Underground.

> First, we ❶descend into an ❷impenetrable ❸darkness, followed by a brief glimpse of feeble daylight; then back into the dark, interrupted every now and then by strange flashes of light; then we emerge into a station lit by hundreds of lamps, only for the station to disappear after a moment.

❶ Verb: suggests a drop or a fall

❷ Adjective: suggests it is impossible to get out of

❸ Noun: has connotations of horror and fear

Now have a go. Select one more verb, adjective and noun from the extract above and use inference to explain the effect. Remember to think about what the words or phrases mean within the text – don't just think about literal meanings.

Verb: _____

_____
_____
_____

Adjective: _____

_____
_____
_____

Noun: _____

_____
_____
_____

AO2 Techniques

When looking at a writer's language choices, you need to consider the use of language techniques such as metaphor, alliteration and personification.

For instance, look at the way the writer's choice of language techniques in this paragraph highlight her feelings that she is out of place at her friend's house. Notice also that the correct terminology has been used for each technique.

> Every ❶crunch and gulp resounded in my head; no chatter cluttered the table. Tamsyn's parents spoke one at a time, in ❷low, luxuriously slow voices. In a corner of the room ❸lurked the television, its screen a black hole.

❶ Onomatopoeia makes her eating sound noisy and rude.

❷ Alliteration links these adjectives, emphasising the wealth and comfort of Tamsyn's home.

❸ The television is personified with the verb 'lurked', suggesting it is dangerous.

Now **have a go** at using inference on some of the word classes and techniques in this extract. Think about how the writer uses language to suggest the narrator feels bullied at school.

> It was like being dropped into one of the wildlife programmes that used to hold my stepfather spellbound in his armchair: fierce cats lurking behind the bushes, muscles poised to pounce on knock-kneed deer.

Question 1. What is the effect of the simile about wildlife programmes?

_____

_____

_____

Question 2. Why has the writer used the metaphor of a fierce cat to describe the bullies?

_____

_____

_____

Beginnings and endings　　　AO2

On Paper 2, one of the AO2 questions will ask you to consider the **structure** of the text. One way to do this is to think about how readers will feel at the beginning and end of the text.

For instance, look at the beginning of an extract about a playground fight that is expected to happen after school.

> The rest of the day was horrendous. ❶I couldn't concentrate. I got a sickening, lurching feeling every time I remembered what was in store once school finished.

❶ The focus on his feelings of fear create empathy for the narrator; readers will perhaps be anxious to find out if he will get badly hurt.

Now **have a go**. Here is the end of the extract about a playground fight. The narrator and his friend feel ashamed that they did not know how to fight properly.

> In a final flurry of shame and humiliation Peter and I came together and I ended up with a black eye and he got a cauliflower ear. Neither of us cried though.

Question 1. How would readers feel about the narrator getting a black eye?

_____
_____
_____

Question 2. How would readers feel after reading that 'neither of us cried'?

_____
_____
_____

Question 3. How would readers feel about Peter?

_____
_____
_____

AO2 — Sentences and punctuation

Sentence style is one of the structural features you need to consider in a text. This includes the length of a sentence and the punctuation used within it.

For instance, look at the use of sentence style and punctuation in this extract about teenagers.

> ❶ Colin and Raymond scowl up at him❷; they are not happy to be here or grateful for their second chance. They look at us clean-haired, well-behaved children in our maroon blazers, starched white shirts and striped ties with contempt.

❶ Both sentences are long and descriptive, and putting them close together in one paragraph creates a clear contrast between the two groups. This creates tension for readers as it creates an atmosphere of danger.

❷ A semi-colon adds extra information about why the boys are not happy; this emphasises how unpleasant they seem.

Now **have a go** at using inference to consider the effect of the sentences and punctuation in this short extract.

> Colin swivels round. Everyone stops chattering and stares at us. I look for a teacher to come and save me but nobody's near so I grip the bench tightly and stare straight back at Colin, waiting for the punch. His mouth twists into a sly smile.

Question 1. Why has the writer started the paragraph with a short sentence and then two longer sentences?

_____
_____
_____

Question 2. Why does the writer use a comma before 'waiting for the punch'?

_____
_____
_____

Techniques and rhetorical devices

AO2

Structural features include repetition of a word or phrase, lists, rhetorical questions, and the rule of three.

You need to use inference to consider their effect.

For instance, look at how the techniques in this extract emphasise the narrator's annoyance about a local restaurant's attempt at authentic Indian cooking.

> One of the dishes listed was Chicken Chuddi, described as an exotic blend of ❶authentic spices, tomato and peppers. It sounded so generic. ❷What was an exotic blend, what were authentic spices, also – ❸tomato and pepper?
> These were the biggest tastemakers aside from chicken in the dish?
> What was Chicken Chuddi?

❶ List in a rule of three makes it sound memorable and perhaps easy to understand.

❷ A series of three rhetorical questions emphasises the writer's growing anger at the lack of real Indian ingredients in the dish.

❸ 'tomato and pepper' are repeated as if to highlight how ordinary they are, also suggesting that they are boring ingredients to have in an 'exotic' dish.

Now **have a go** at using inference to consider the effect of some other structural features in the extract above.

Question 1. What is the effect of repeating the word 'exotic'?

_____
_____
_____

Question 2. Why has the writer used a rhetorical question about 'Chicken Chuddi' at the end of the extract?

_____
_____
_____

AO2 — Paper 1 language question

Paper 1 language questions ask you to comment on the writer's language choices in text 1.

❶ This question is language only, it is not asking you to look at structure.

❷ Think about what is interesting and informative about the text, and what words and techniques are used to make it interesting.

> How does the writer use ❶language to ❷interest and inform the reader?
>
> You should include:
>
> - The writer's use of language
> - The ❸effect on the reader
>
> ❹Use examples from the ❺whole text and relevant subject terminology.

❸ Use inference to consider the effect of the language you select.

❹ Use short, embedded quotations and explain their effect. Try to use the correct terminology for your examples.

❺ The Paper 1 AO2 question will ask you to look at the whole of text 1, so you need to read the text carefully before you start your answer to ensure you have fully understood all the writer's ideas.

Now **have a go**. Look at text D 'Flowing Hair for Ladies' on page 96.

Question 1. Highlight at least two words, phrases or techniques you think are interesting or informative and use inference to explain their effect.

_____

_____

_____

_____

_____

Question 2. Can you add subject terminology to your examples?

Paper 2 language question

AO2

Paper 2 will have one question based on a short extract from text 1.

> Colin and Raymond scowl up at him; they are not happy to be here or grateful for their second chance. They look at us clean-haired, well-behaved children in our maroon blazers, starched white shirts and striped ties with contempt. Their holey grey socks were crumpled around their ankles, they don't wear silly short-shorts like all the other boys in my class – their shorts are long, right down to their scabby knees. They have greasy brown fringes hanging in their eyes.

How does the writer use ❶language to ❷present Colin and Raymond? Use ❸examples from the extract and subject terminology.

❶ This question is language only, it is not asking you to look at structure.

❷ The question has a clear focus so only select language which you can link to this focus.

❸ Use short, embedded quotations and explain their effect. Try to use the correct terminology for your examples.

Now **have a go**. Read the short above extract carefully.

Question 1. Which of the following words best describes the way Colin and Raymond are presented? Circle your answer.

Smart | Threatening | Immature | Scruffy

Question 2. Find **two** words, phrases or techniques from the short extract in the question that you can link to the word you chose above. Use inference to explain the effect.

- _____
  _____
  _____

- _____
  _____
  _____

AO2 Paper 2 language and structure question

Paper 2 will have one question based on the whole of text 2.

① Select interesting and engaging language by thinking about what ideas are in the text, rather than just looking at obvious techniques.

② This question is language **and** structure, so remember to consider the overall structure of the texts as well as language and structural techniques.

How does the writer try to **①**interest and engage the reader?

You should include:

- The writer's use of **②**language
- The writer's use of **②**structure
- The **③**effect on the reader

④Use examples from the **⑤**whole text and relevant subject terminology.

③ Use inference to consider the effect of the language you select.

④ Use short, embedded quotations and explain their effect. Try to use the correct terminology for your examples.

⑤ This question asks you to look at the whole of text 2, so you need to read the text carefully before you start your answer to ensure you have fully understood all the writer's ideas.

Now have a go. Look at text J 'The Hate U Give' on page 102.

Question 1. Look at the opening paragraph of the text. Select **two** interesting words or techniques and explain their effect.

_____
_____
_____

Question 2. Look at the beginning and then the ending of the text – how will they make readers feel?

_____
_____
_____

20

Paper 1 practice

AO2

Read text C 'Memories of London' on page **95** about travelling on the underground. Then look at the question below and the first paragraph from a student answer. The student has focused on the first of the writer's ideas in the text.

> How does the writer use language to interest and inform the reader?
>
> You should include:
> - The writer's use of language
> - The effect on the reader
>
> Use examples from the whole text and relevant subject terminology.

❶ There is a focus on the question at the start, with a clear understanding shown of the ideas in the text.

❷ Some subject terminology has been used but remember to focus on the effect rather than just identifying obvious language features.

> ❶ The writer interests the reader in his journey by suggesting that he is literally taken to another world using the ❷ verb "❸ transported". He then makes the journey seem even more magical but also a bit frightening by writing of the 'night' and using the adjective 'flickering' ❹ which has connotations of danger. This danger is emphasised by personification of the light as 'feeble' which suggests it is weak and helpless.

❸ Quotations are short and embedded, which makes it easier to focus on the effect of the word or phrase.

❹ Inference is used to consider the effect of each of the language examples.

Now **have a go**. The writer goes on to describe the journey in more detail. Write a paragraph explaining how he uses language to make it seem exciting. Use a separate piece of paper if necessary.

_____
_____
_____
_____
_____

AO2 Paper 2 practice

Read text L 'About a Boy' on page 104. Then look at the question below and the first paragraph from a student answer. The student has focused on the first of the writer's ideas in the text and it engages the reader from the start.

> How does the writer try to interest and engage the reader?
>
> You should include:
> - The writer's use of language
> - The writer's use of structure
> - The effect on the reader
>
> Use examples from the whole text and relevant subject terminology.

① There is a focus on the question at the start, with a clear understanding shown of the way the writer engages the reader.

② Subject terminology has been used, but the language and structure examples have been selected as they all show how Marcus feels, they are not just a selection of obvious techniques.

> **①** The writer engages the reader by showing us how Marcus feels, starting with a **②** rule of three in the first sentence **③** to emphasise his sensible behaviour, like getting there 'early' and going straight to his desk. **④** A short sentence is then used to focus the reader on his fear as he is only 'safe enough', which suggests he is in the safest place he can find, but is still scared. His fear is highlighted again with the adverb 'darkly' which has connotations of danger. **⑤** This opening would make readers have sympathy for Marcus as it contrasts him with the bullies who are 'smoking'.

③ Inference is used to consider the effect of all the examples selected.

④ The effect of a short sentence is then explained.

⑤ The structure of the extract is covered, with a focus on the effect of the opening of the text.

Now have a go. The writer goes on to describe why he is bullied. Write a paragraph explaining how he uses language and structure to engage the reader's sympathy. Use a separate piece of paper for your answer.

Top tips and practice   AO2

Top tips:

- Read the extract carefully before starting to answer the questions.
- Select interesting language, not just obvious language features.
- Always explain the effect of your examples.
- Embed short quotations rather than copying out whole sentences.
- When asked to consider structure, always start with how the text begins, and how it ends.

Challenge:

Have a go at the following AO2 questions. Read the extracts carefully, then write your answers on a separate piece of paper.

Read text A 'Bathing in the River' on page **93**. Remember this would be worth **8** marks in the exam, so you should be aiming for two or three short paragraphs.

> How does the writer use language to interest and inform the reader?
>
> You should include:
> - The writer's use of language
> - The effect on the reader
>
> Use examples from the **whole text** and relevant subject terminology.

Read text K 'Clothes, clothes, clothes, music, music, music, boys, boys, boys' on page **103**. Remember this would be worth **10** marks in the exam, so you should be aiming for three paragraphs.

> The writer presents a memory from her school days.
>
> How does the writer try to interest and engage the reader?
>
> You should include:
> - The writer's use of language
> - The writer's use of structure
> - The effect on the reader
>
> Use examples from the **whole text** and relevant subject terminology.

AO3

Compare writers' ideas and perspectives, as well as how these are conveyed, across two or more texts.

Question style

AO3 will assess your ability to compare. 'Compare' means to consider the ways in which two things are similar, and the ways in which they are different.

For instance, the question will ask you to compare the two reading texts in Paper 2.

❶ 'Ideas' means the main points the writer uses in the text.

❷ 'Perspective' and 'points of view' means the way the writer feels about the ideas he/she uses.

❸ The questions will have a focus. In this question it is 'school', so you should concentrate on the parts of the text that are relevant to the writers' experiences at school.

> Compare the writers' ❶ideas and ❷perspectives about ❸school.
>
> You should compare the:
> - ❶main ideas
> - ❷points of view
> - ❹presentation of these ideas and views.
>
> ❺Use examples from ❻both texts to support your comparison.

❹ 'Presentation' means the way the writers show their ideas through the language and structure of the text.

❺ Your examples can be short quotations or paraphrases, but you do not have to use subject terminology.

❻ You must use examples from both texts.

Now **have a go**. Decide whether the following statements are **True** or **False**. Circle the correct answers.

- Evidence must be a short quotation. **True / False**
- Comparisons must be about everything in the texts. **True / False**
- Subject terminology must be used. **True / False**

24

Identifying perspectives   AO3

AO3 will ask you to compare the writer's points of view, or their 'perspectives'. This means using inference to consider how they feel about the topic they are writing about. One way to approach this is to think about whether they present the topic as negative or positive.

For instance, look at the focus in this comparison question. Notice how inference can be used to consider the writer's perspective.

> Compare the writers' ideas and perspectives about working with machinery.
>
> > Machines with their own small motors started with a ❶jerk and a whine under the shadows of their operators, increasing a noise that ❶made the brain reel and ache…

❶ The writer seems to be negative about machinery, as the machines are noisy and the phrase 'brain reel and ache' suggests this is actually painful.

Now **have a go**. Look again at the comparison question above and the start of another text about working with machinery. Decide whether the perspective is positive or negative and then finish the sentence, using the example above as a model.

> Trucks backed in. We swung our hooks. Haul, hoist, pull, push. Stack on pallets. Forklift slides in, lifts the load, reverses, stacks the load in the warehouse, and back to the platform. You worked with your body and your brain had a day off.

The writer seems to be [positive | negative] about working with machinery, as …

_____

_____

AO3 Identifying ideas

AO3 will ask you to compare the writer's main ideas. A good place to start is to identify what ideas the two texts have in common.

For instance, look at the focus in this comparison question. Notice the ideas that they have in common.

Compare the writer's ideas and perspectives about work.

Robboe the foreman bent over a stack of new timesheets behind his glass partition; ❶women and girls wearing turbans and hair-nets and men and boys in clean blue overalls, settled down to their work, ❷eager to get a good start on their day's stint…

❶You learned the ways of truckers and their helpers. Independent truckers were easy. They worked for themselves, set their own pace. ❷Corporation truckers prodded you to hurry up, man, lift the […] load, let's go.

---

❶ Both work with others

❷ Both work with people who want to work quickly

Now **have a go**. Read the whole of text G 'Saturday Night and Sunday Morning' on page **99** and Text H 'Teacher Man' on page **100**. Identify **three** more ideas they have in common.

Both _____

_____

_____

Both _____

_____

_____

Both _____

_____

_____

Comparing ideas and perspectives

AO3

When you have identified ideas and perspectives that are relevant to the focus of the comparison question, you need to consider how they are similar or different. To do this, you should use appropriate connective words and phrases.

For instance, look this table of connective words and phrases that could be used to create a comparative paragraph.

Adding an example	**For example**, the writer of text one says …
	For instance, in text two the writer …
Comparing or contrasting	**Both** texts….
	Similarly, the writer of text two feels
	However, text two seems to be saying …
	Likewise, the writer of text one …
	In contrast, text two …
	On the other hand, in text two …
Using inference	This **suggests** …
	This **implies** …
	This **reflects** …

Now **have a go**. Read this paragraph comparing the writers' perspectives about working with machinery and add appropriate connective phrases from the table above.

_____ writers describe their feelings about working with machinery. _____, in text 1, Sillitoe describes the machines as starting with 'a jerk and a whine' which makes the 'brain reel and ache'. This _____ his perspective is negative, as the work causes actual physical pain. _____, McCourt seems positive about his work. He says that 'your brain had a day off' which _____ he did not have to think much about it.

A03 Comparing the writers' language

When you compare the writers' ideas and perspectives, you need to consider **how** they are presented. One way is to consider the similarities and differences in the language of the two texts.

For instance, look at these extracts from two texts about childhood. Both are about the way the young girls feel out of place amongst their friends, and the annotations explore similarities and differences in the way these feelings are presented.

> Or I could call Hailey and Maya, those girls Kenya claims ❶don't count as my friends. I guess I can see why she says that. I never invite them over. Why would I? They live in mini-mansions. My house is just mini.

> ❷Every crunch and gulp resounded in my head; no chatter cluttered the table. Tamsyn's parents spoke one at a time, in low, luxuriously slow voices.

❶ Colloquial informal language makes her seem young and vulnerable.

❷ The writer is also self-conscious but it is highlighted through the harsh verbs used to describe the way she eats.

Now **have a go**. Look again at the short extracts above and then complete the comparison below.

> The writer of text 1 suggests the narrator is embarrassed about her house as she uses alliteration to describe her friend's houses as 'mini-mansions', then calls her own 'mini' to highlight how small it is. The writer of text 2 also seems embarrassed as she…

Comparing the writers' structure

AO3

When you compare the writers' ideas and perspectives, you need to consider **how** they are presented. One way is to consider the similarities and differences in the structure of the two texts.

For instance, look at these extracts from two texts about childhood. Both are about the way the writers feel out of place amongst their friends, but they structure their ideas differently.

> Or I could call Hailey and Maya, those girls Kenya claims don't count as my friends. I guess I can see why she says that. I never invite them over. ❶Why would I? They live in mini-mansions. My house is just mini.

> ❷ The tablecloth was white lace. Every crunch and gulp resounded in my head; no chatter cluttered the table. Tamsyn's parents spoke one at a time, in low, luxuriously slow voices.

❶ The rhetorical question suggests she knows she is not accepted and is trying to be brave

❷ Everything is described in detail which slows down the pace, emphasising the many ways she feels out of place.

Now **have a go**. Look again at the short extracts above about childhood. Both use sentence structure to emphasise the girls' feelings.

Question 1. Text 1 uses _____

_____

Text 2 uses _____

_____

Question 2. Are the sentence styles similar or different? Circle your answer.

Question 3. Write a few sentences explaining your choice.

_____
_____
_____
_____
_____

AO3 Comparison question practice

Read text K 'Clothes, clothes, clothes, music, music, music, boys, boys, boys' on page **103** and text L 'About a Boy' on page **104**, then look at the question below.

> Compare the writers' ideas and perspectives about their school.
>
> You should compare the:
> - main ideas
> - points of view
> - presentation of these ideas and views.
>
> Use examples from both texts to support your comparison.

Now read this paragraph from the start of a student's answer. The student has focused on the writers' perspectives of their schooldays.

> **❶**Both writers describe their **❷**feelings about events from their schooldays. For instance, in text 1, the writer seems to feel positive about her schooldays **❹**as she starts by suggesting Colin and Raymond are exciting as they do not wear **❸**'silly short-shorts' like her friends. In contrast the start of text two suggests Marcus' negative feelings about school as the writer describes him arriving early in order to miss the other kids who have bullied him.

❶ Connective words and phrases used.

❷ The focus of the question is clearly addressed.

❸ Evidence in the form of short quotations and paraphrases, is used from **both** texts.

❹ The presentation is compared through the differences in structure.

Now **have a go**. Read the question and the extracts again carefully.

Both writers go on to describe the behaviour of people at school. Write a paragraph comparing the way the writers' present this idea. You could compare the differences in language. Use a separate piece of paper if necessary.

_____
_____
_____
_____
_____

Top tips and practice

AO3

Top tips:

- Read the question carefully so that you can stick to the focus.
- Identify the writer' perspectives about the topic in the question.
- Identify two or three ideas that the texts have in common.
- Consider the different ways the writers present their ideas and perspectives through language and structure.
- Use connective words or phrases to create comparative paragraphs.
- Use evidence from both texts.

Challenge:

Have a go at the following comparative question. Read the extracts carefully first, and then write your answer on a separate piece of paper. Remember the question would be worth **16** marks, so it is worth aiming for at least three comparative paragraphs. You could use the space around the question to plan your answer.

Read text G 'Saturday Night and Sunday Morning' on page **99** and text H 'Teacher Man' on page **100** and answer the question below.

> Compare the writers' ideas and perspectives about work.
>
> You should compare the:
>
> - main ideas
> - points of view
> - presentation of these ideas and views.
>
> Use examples from both texts to support your comparison.

AO4 Evaluate texts critically and support this with appropriate textual references.

Question style

AO4 will assess your ability to evaluate the ideas and opinions of the writer. 'Evaluate' means to consider how well something is achieved and to give your judgement.

For instance, the questions will ask you to evaluate the success of the 19th century texts you read for Paper 1.

> In ❶lines 1 to 9 the writer ❷tries to persuade readers that giving to charity is worthwhile.
>
> Evaluate how successfully this is achieved.
>
> Give ❸three reasons for your opinion and ❹use examples from lines 1 to 9.

> For this question refer to the ❺whole of text 2.
>
> 'In my view, this text makes me feel ❷that some people really deserve charity'.
>
> Based on your evaluation of the text, ❻how far do you agree with this opinion?
>
> ❹Use examples from the text to support your evaluation.

❶ If questions use a short extract or give line numbers, look in these parts for your answer.

❷ The questions will have a focus. Concentrate on the parts that relate to the focus.

❸ Number of answers needed is clearly shown.

❹ Use evidence to support your judgements. This can be short quotations or paraphrases.

❺ One question will ask you to look at the whole of a text.

❻ These questions are worth more marks, so you think about 'how far' you agree or disagree.

Now **have a go**. Decide whether the following statements are **True** or **False**. Circle the correct answers.

- Evidence must be a short quotation. **True / False**
- Evidence must always be taken from the whole of a text. **True / False**
- Evaluate means making a judgement. **True / False**

Evaluation

AO4

'Evaluate' means to consider how well something is achieved and to give your judgement. It is not enough to say whether you like or dislike it, you must base your judgement on the ideas in the text. You must also use examples from the text to support your judgement.

You do not need to explain a writer's language or structure choices. A useful way to approach evaluation questions is to consider the writer's intentions and how they have achieved this intention with the ideas, opinions and viewpoints they have used.

For instance, this writer has a very strong viewpoint about bad manners. Look at the ideas and opinions he uses to back up his viewpoint.

> Never criticize any dish before you. If a dish is distasteful to you, decline it, but make no remarks about it. It is ❶sickening and disgusting to explain at a table how one article makes you sick, or why some other dish has become distasteful to you. I have seen a well-dressed tempting dish go from a table untouched, ❷because one of the company told a most disgusting anecdote about finding vermin served in a similar dish. No wit in the narration can excuse so palpably an error of politeness.
>
> Never use your knife for any purpose but to cut your food. It is not meant to be put in your mouth. Your fork is intended to carry the food from your plate to your mouth, and no gentleman ever eats with his knife.

❶ The writer feels that it is 'sickening and disgusting' to criticise food you are given, this helps readers to understand why such behaviour is bad manners.

❷ The writer uses an anecdote about rudeness during a meal which would be helpful as a real example of bad manners.

Now **have a go**. The writer gives more views about bad manners in the final paragraph, including his opinion about the way cutlery is used. What is his viewpoint about the way cutlery should be used?

_____
_____
_____
_____
_____
_____
_____

A04 Finding relevant ideas

When evaluating, you should consider the focus of the question and read the text carefully to find ideas, opinions or viewpoints that are relevant.

For instance, look at this question about train travel, and the two parts of the text which a student felt were relevant to the focus of the question.

> In this extract, the writer tries to persuade readers to travel by train.
>
> Evaluate how successfully this is achieved.
>
> Give **three** reasons for your opinion and use examples from the extract.
>
> > <u>The third-class ticket gives you quite as good a chance, perhaps a better one, of being pushed into a first-class carriage</u>, and in whatever class of carriage you may happen to be carried into by the excited throngs who "rush" the swiftly-succeeding trains, you will find much the same kind of crowded company. In all classes <u>I have been nearly smothered</u>, as it were between feather-beds, by plump matrons. Of course, trodden-on-toes don't count. Everybody treads on everybody else's toes. The ride, however, is not a long one, and if you only keep your temper – do not give yourself airs – you may get a good deal of fun instead of annoyance out of the universal "squeege".
>
>
>
> This is an idea about ticket types, so it is relevant to the question.
>
> This an opinion about what it is like to travel by train, so it is relevant to the question.

Now **have a go**.

Read the above extract again. Find and underline one more idea, opinion or viewpoint that the writer uses to try and persuade readers to travel by train. Write your explanation below.

_____
_____

Explaining relevant ideas

AO4

Before making a judgement about a text, you need to use inference to explain the ideas, opinions or viewpoints you have chosen. You also need to use evidence which can be either short quotations or a paraphrase.

For instance, look at the student's explanation below in response to a question about train travel.

> In this extract, the writer tries to persuade readers to travel by train.
> Evaluate how successfully this is achieved.
>
>> In all classes I have been nearly smothered, as it were between feather-beds, by plump matrons. Of course, trodden-on-toes don't count. Everybody treads on everybody else's toes. The ride, however, is not a long one, and if you only keep your temper – do not give yourself airs – you may get a good deal of fun instead of annoyance out of the universal "squeege".

The writer says that ❶ he has often been 'smothered' ❷ which suggests that train travel can be uncomfortable.

❶ A mixture of short quotations and paraphrase has been used as evidence for the idea.

❷ Inference is used in the explanation and made clear with the phrase 'this suggests'.

Now **have a go.**

Two more quotations in the text have been underlined for you. Select one to discuss a new idea the writer uses to persuade readers to travel by train and use inference in an explanation. Remember to use a short quotation or paraphrase as evidence of the idea.

The writer says …

_____

Which suggests …

_____
_____

AO4 Making a judgement

Evaluating means assessing something and coming to a judgement about its value. When you evaluate a text, you should assess **how well** the writer's ideas achieve the purpose of the text. To do this, you should think about the readers of the texts, and how they will feel.

For instance, look at the student's evaluation made in response to this question about train travel. The student:

❶ identifies – and underlines – a relevant idea

❷ uses inference to explain it

❸ judges how well it persuades readers (the word 'because' is useful as it explains the reason behind the judgement).

> In this extract, the writer tries to persuade readers to travel by train.
>
> Evaluate how successfully this is achieved.
>
> > ❶ <u>In all classes I have been nearly smothered</u>, as it were between feather-beds, by plump matrons. Of course, trodden-on-toes don't count. Everybody treads on everybody else's toes. The ride, however, is not a long one …

❷ The writer describes being 'nearly smothered' which suggests trains are over-crowded.

❸ This would not persuade readers to travel by train because it sounds uncomfortable and claustrophobic.

Now have a go. Read the question and the text again carefully. Use the example above as a model to complete the following evaluation.

> The writer says that 'the ride' is 'not a long one' which suggests that trains are fast and speedy. This would persuade readers to travel by train because …
>
> _____
> _____
> _____

Short extract practice

A04

Read text F 'Manners' on page **98**, then look at the question below.

> In lines 14 to 22 the writer tries to persuade readers of the importance of good table manners.
>
> Evaluate how successfully this is achieved.
>
> Give **three** reasons for your opinion and use examples from lines 14 to 22.

Now read this paragraph from a student response. It covers one of the reasons needed for the full answer.

> The writer expresses the ❶opinion that ❷making comments about food you are given is 'sickening'. ❸This suggests that such behaviour is rude to your hosts and would ❹successfully persuade people because most people want to behave politely to others.

❶ The student has selected a relevant opinion from the text.

❷ The evidence is a combination of quotation and paraphrase.

❸ The student has used inference in a clear explanation.

❹ The student has made a judgement, using the word 'because'.

Now **have a go.** Read the question and the extract again carefully. Use the example above as a model to give two more reasons in response to the question. Use a separate piece of paper if necessary.

_____
_____
_____
_____
_____
_____
_____

A04 Whole text (part 1)

One evaluation question on Paper 1 will ask you to evaluate the whole of a longer 19th century text. You will be asked how far you agree with an opinion about the effectiveness of the whole text. It is a good idea to start your answer by giving an overview of your opinion.

For instance, in answer to the following question about text F 'Manners' on page 98, two students have started their answer with an overview.

> For this question refer to the whole of text F.
>
> 'In my view, this text really shows how offensive bad manners can be.'
>
> Based on your evaluation of the text, how far do you agree with this opinion?

> Overall I agree with this statement because the writer makes bad manners sound really disgusting to watch.

> I both agree and disagree with the statement because the writer does make bad manners sound really disgusting, but he also uses exaggerated examples which sound immature.

Now **have a go**. Read the whole of text C 'Memories of London' on page 95. Then, write an overview sentence giving your opinion about this statement from a whole text evaluation question.

> 'In my view, this makes travelling on the train sound really exciting.'

_____
_____
_____
_____

Whole text (part 2)

AO4

When evaluating the whole of a text, you need to select ideas from across the whole extract. You should also develop your evaluations. You can do this by considering a range of reader responses.

For instance, read text F 'Manners' on page **98** and this statement from a whole text evaluation question.

> 'In my view, this text really shows how offensive bad manners can be.'

A student has selected a relevant idea and considered more than one type of reader response.

> I agree with the statement because the writer makes his feelings about manners clear by using several personal examples of bad table manners that he has seen. For instance, he uses exaggerated examples about men who might suffocate or choke if they fill their mouths too full, which shows how offensive the behaviour is. This might make readers stop and think about their own behaviour before they eat. ❶However, some readers may find the exaggeration a bit immature, and this might cause them to ignore the advice.

❶ This answer is developed with an evaluation of the way some readers might not be persuaded by the examples the writer uses.

Now **have a go**.

Question 1. Read the whole of text F 'Manners' on page **98**. Find another idea that is relevant to the statement about how offensive bad manners can be.

_____

_____

Question 2. Write a developed evaluation by considering more than one possible reader response. Use a separate piece of paper if you need more space.

_____

_____

AO4 Whole text practice

Read text E 'The Moustache' on page 97, then look at the question below.

> For this question refer to the whole the text.
>
> 'In my view, this text makes a moustache sounds like something every young man should have'.
>
> Based on your evaluation of the text, how far do you agree with this opinion?
>
> Use examples from the text to support your evaluation.

Now read this paragraph where a student evaluates one reason from the text.

> Overall, **❶I agree with this opinion** as the writer starts the text by making a joke about needing **❷a 'microscope' to see smaller moustaches**. **❸This suggests that men without moustaches are going to be laughed at**, which would **❹help to persuade young men to grow one so that they fit in with their friends. However, this jokey tone might put some men off as they might find it a bit immature, and young men like to be taken seriously**.

❶ A relevant opinion from the text has been selected

❷ The evidence is a combination of quotation and paraphrase.

❸ Inference is used in a clear explanation

❹ This evaluation is developed with ideas that are 'for' and 'against' the statement in the question.

Now have a go. Carefully read the question and the extract on page 97 again. Use the example above as a model to evaluate the ideas and opinions in the rest of the text. Use a separate piece of paper if necessary.

_____
_____
_____
_____
_____

Top tips and practice — AO4

Top tips:

- Find ideas or opinions in the text that are relevant to the question.
- Use inference to explain the ideas you have found.
- Make a judgement about how successfully the idea or opinion fulfils the writer's intentions.
- Use short, embedded quotations or paraphrase the text as evidence.
- When writing about a whole text, develop your response by considering a range of reader responses.
- Don't write about the effect of words and phrases, think about the writer's intentions and ideas.

Challenge:

Have a go at the following evaluation questions. Read text B 'Baths by the Sea' on page 94, then write your answer on a separate piece of paper. Remember that the second question is worth double the marks of the first.

> In this extract, the writer tries to offer advice about sea bathing.
>
>> I do not advise any girl to begin bathing the very first day of her arrival at the seaside. Better she should spend this day loitering on the sands or among the rocks, where, if she has any taste for the beautiful, she will find a thousand and one objects to interest her. Indeed, at the seaside one cannot be too much out of doors, and as for children they may with benefit paddle about among the wavelets, or build sand castles all day long. Avoid parties and concerts while on your maritime holiday. Your pleasures ought to be of the very quietest nature possible.
>
> Evaluate how successfully this is achieved.

> Give **three** reasons for your opinion and use examples from the extract.
> For this question refer to the whole of text B.
> 'In my view, this text makes swimming in the sea sound very healthy.'
> Based on your evaluation of the text, how far do you agree with this opinion?
> Use examples from the text to support your evaluation.

AO5

Communicate clearly, effectively and imaginatively, selecting and adapting tone, style and register for different forms, purposes and audience.

Transactional writing | Plan Unlock the question

AO5 **Transactional writing** questions appear on Paper 1. The questions will test your ability to write for a variety of different audiences and purposes. First, you need to unlock the question by thinking carefully about both the purpose and the audience for the writing. Consider what your audience needs to know, and what will specifically appeal to them.

For instance, have a look at the annotations for the questions below.

❶ Purpose: A review, so this needs to be engaging, but informative. It also needs to give practical information about places to go.

❷ Audience: Young adults, so the review needs to focus on what they would be interested in. Write about both sport and entertainment, as well as good fast-food places.

> 'Come and visit. You might be surprised!'
>
> Using this title, write a ❶review of your hometown. The review will be published on a website for ❷young adults.

❶ Purpose: A speech, so this needs an engaging opening and a pacy style. It also needs a strong ending that persuades them to sign up to something soon.

❷ Audience: People of your age or friendship group, so the speech needs to address them directly. Think about what they already do and how they can use that for charity. Also think about what charities appeal to them.

> Write a ❶speech to be given to your ❷peer group with the title: 'Charity work makes you feel good'.

Now **have a go** at unlocking this question by annotating it with ideas about the audience and purpose. Use a separate piece of paper if you need more space.

> Write an article for a national newspaper with the title 'How to be a good friend'.

Plan Gathering ideas

AO5

Before starting your answer to a transactional writing question, you should spend around **10 minutes** planning. One way to gather ideas for your plan is to spend a minute or two writing down everything you can think of that might be appropriate. This is called 'thought association'.

For instance, look at these ideas that a student has gathered for a question about technology.

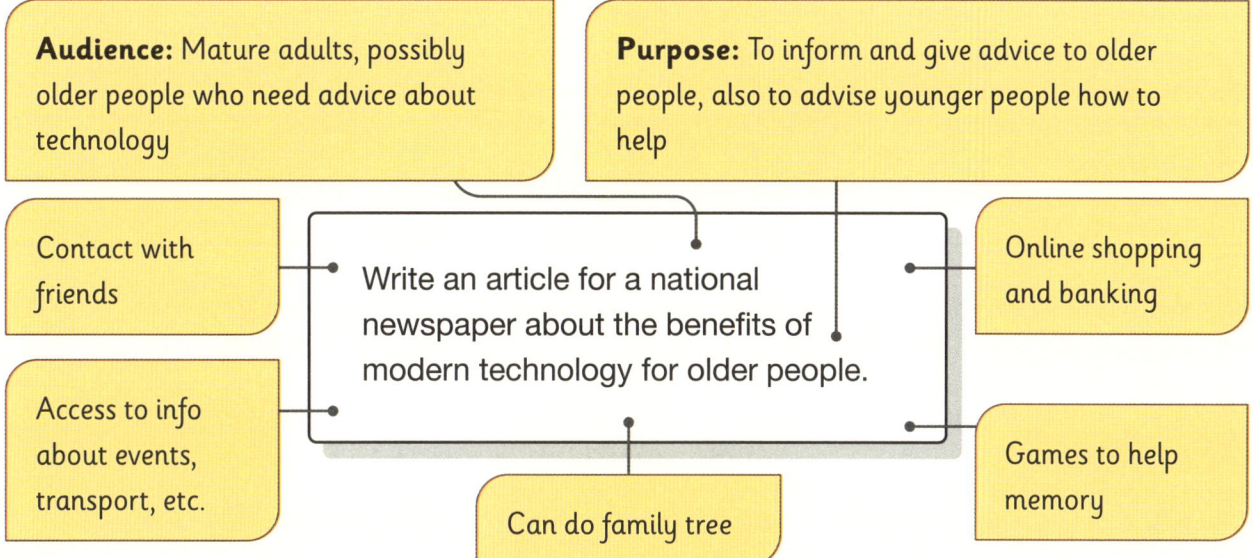

Now **have a go** at using thought association for the following question. Use a separate piece of paper if you need more space.

> Write an article for a national newspaper with the title 'Every 16 year-old should have a part-time job'.

A05 Plan Using the question (part 1)

Before starting your answer to a transactional writing question, you should spend around **10** minutes planning. One way to do this is to use the question. One of the questions has an opening paragraph that gives a few prompts to help you gather ideas.

For instance, look at this question about appearance. The student has used the prompts in the question to start a plan.

Audience: Mostly mature, could also be teenagers so address them directly.

Purpose: To argue and inform, needs to be formal but also entertaining.

Damage to mental health, high anxiety, lack of confidence.

Write a speech for a local radio station with the title 'How important is looking good?'

A student has started a response to this task. Continue this speech using your own ideas.

We all know the damage done by unrealistic social media posts. We all know that we should try not to judge others on appearance alone. But I'm here to tell you that there are still occasions when looking good is important.'

We don't know what someone is really like inside.

Job interviews, weddings, school/college uniform.

Now **have a go** at using thought association to add a few more ideas.

- _____
- _____
- _____
- _____

Now cross out any ideas you think are not suitable for the audience, or you do not think you can develop fully.

Plan Using the question (part 2) — AO5

Before starting your answer to a transactional writing question, you should spend around 10 minutes planning. One way to do this is to use the question. One of the questions has three bullet points that can be used as prompts to generate ideas.

For instance, look at this question about exams. The student has used the prompts in the question to start a plan.

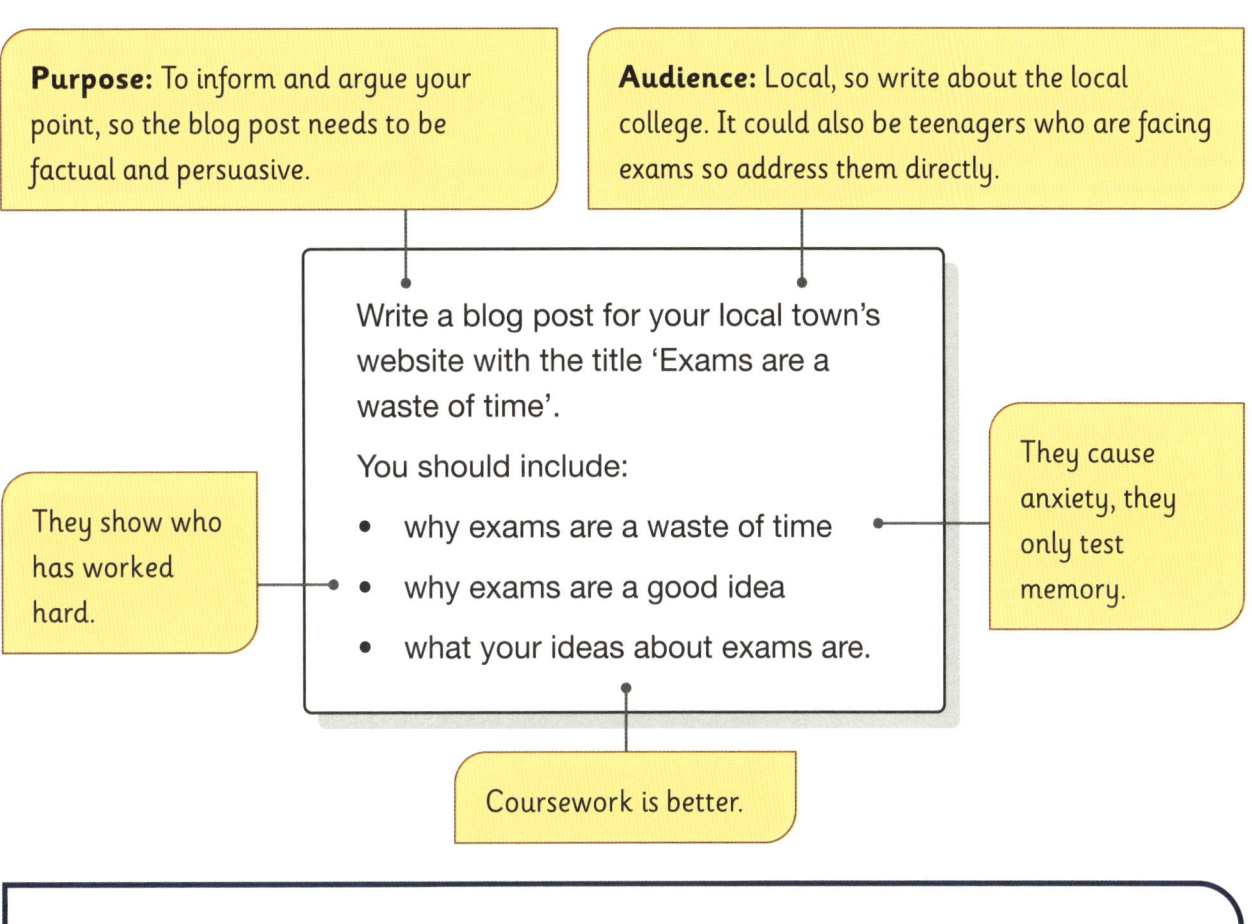

Now **have a go** at using thought association to add a few more ideas.

- _____
- _____
- _____
- _____

Now cross out any ideas you think are not suitable for the audience, or you do not think you can develop fully.

A05 Plan Top tips and practice

Top tips:

- Read the question carefully before starting your answer.
- Annotate the question with ideas about the audience and purpose.
- Use thought association to come up with ideas.
- Use the idea prompts in the question.
- Read through your ideas and cross out any which are not appropriate for your audience and purpose.

Now **have a go** at gathering ideas for the following question.

> Write a letter to your local newspaper about a proposal to ban music festivals in the local park.
>
> You should include:
>
> - reasons why the ban is good idea
> - reasons why festivals should be allowed
> - your views on local music festivals
>
> Use a separate piece of paper if you need more space.

Structure Overall structure AO5

As part of your planning process, you need to plan the overall structure of your answer. This means thinking carefully about the order in which you present your ideas.

For instance, look at this question about driving. The student has made notes about audience and purpose and come up with paragraph ideas in a plan.

Audience: Mature readers. Needs to be formal but I can address them directly and be myself.

Purpose: To persuade, using facts and my own opinions.

Write a letter to a national newspaper giving your views about a proposal to raise the minimum driving age to 21.

❶ Strong opening to engage the reader as it shows the issue is personal.

❶ Opening	Introduce myself as a potential young driver who needs a car for work.
❷ Paragraph 1	Benefits of young people driving, creates independence, can get to jobs/college.
Paragraph 2	Disadvantages of young drivers, high accident rates, expensive insurance.
❸ Paragraph 3	My solution – supervised driving for first two years.

❷ The strongest idea has been put first to plant it firmly in the readers' minds.

❸ Ends with a solution, leaves reader with something sensible to think about.

Now **have a go** at answering the following questions about structure.

Question 1. Why is it important to plan for the structure of your writing?

_____

Question 2. Why is it important to think carefully about the opening of your writing?

_____

Question 3. Circle the best way to end your writing.

| With a summary of your previous ideas | With something strong for readers to think about | With 'yours sincerely' |

47

A05 Structure: Ordering your ideas

As part of your planning process, you should think about the order in which you want to present your ideas. You need to use a logical order which guides your reader sensibly through your ideas.

For instance, look at this question about looking good on a budget. Notice that the student has used the opening paragraph as a prompt for four ideas.

Audience: My peers, so informal and colloquial with some humour.

Purpose: To entertain but it needs to be informative and give useful tips.

Write a speech for an audience of your peers with the title 'How to look good on a budget'.

A student has started a response to this task. Continue this speech using your own ideas.

'Social media has increased the pressure on young people to look good. But if you feel left behind due to a lack of finances, I'm here to help. Believe it or not, there are a few simple steps you can take that mean you can be a fashion icon without breaking the bank.'

- Go to charity shops or online outlet shops.
- Learn to sew and alter stuff you already own.
- Share clothes with friends or siblings.
- Get a part-time job to increase your income.

Now **have a go** at adding structure to the plan.

Question 1. If you only had time to use three of the ideas, which one would you discard? Explain your choice.

_____
_____
_____

Question 2. Which order is most logical for the three ideas? Number them 1–3 and write a few sentences explaining the order you have chosen.

_____
_____
_____
_____

Structure Openings

A05

If no opening paragraph is provided in the question, you should think carefully about how to engage your readers from the start of your writing. To do this you need to start with a strong idea and use a technique that will grab their attention.

For instance, look at these openings to a speech about how to look good on a budget.

> **1** Want to be a fashion icon but lack the fashion icon budget? Stick with me and I'll talk you through how to look good without breaking the bank.
>
> **2** 95% of the gorgeous stuff you see people wearing online is only worn once. If you listen to me carefully, I'll tell you how to get hold of it for free.
>
> **3** Rather than constantly wanting more new stuff, you could listen to me and find out how to look good without spending a penny.

1 A rhetorical question

2 A shocking or interesting fact

3 A strong statement or point of view

Now **have a go**. Using one of the above openings as a model, write the opening paragraph to the following question about driving ages.

> Write a letter to a national newspaper giving your views about a proposal to raise the minimum driving age to 21.

A05 Structure Endings

As part of the planning process, you should think carefully about how to end your writing. Your final paragraph, or conclusion, needs to leave your reader with a lasting impression. It is often a good idea to remind them of your strongest idea.

For instance, look at these three ways to end an article about avoiding examination stress.

① Imagine a stressed student sitting alone in their bedroom, aimlessly scrolling through social media. Don't let that be you.

② Some stress is natural, but unless you find a way to deal with it long-term, it can cause serious physical harm.

③ So, look around you at the teenagers facing exams and ask yourself what you can do to help them deal with their stress.

① End with a vivid image

② End with a warning

③ End with a request for action

Now **have a go**. Look at these three ways to end a letter of application for a job in a hotel and then answer the question that follows.

④ My experience means I would be completely at home behind your reception desk, welcoming guests with a warm friendly smile.

⑤ I know you will be seeing other applicants, but you will regret not giving me an opportunity to show you my skills.

⑥ I hope my experience and qualifications are of interest to you, and I would appreciate the opportunity to meet you to discuss the role in more detail.

④ End with a request for action

⑤ End with a warning

⑥ End with a strong image

The audience for this letter would be the manager of the hotel. Which ending do you think is most appropriate for the audience and purpose? Write a sentence explaining your choice.

Structure Top tips and practice — AO5

Top tips:
- Structure your ideas into a logical order.
- If no opening is provided, use an appropriate technique to grab your reader's attention from the start.
- Plan your conclusion to leave your reader with a strong lasting impression.

Now **have a go** at answering the following question. The plan has been started for you. Use a separate piece of paper for your response. Start by structuring the the student's plan by numbering their notes **1** to **3**. Then write one or two sentences that would leave your reader with a lasting impression.

> Brings communities together, helps people who are lonely or disabled.

Write a speech for your peers with the title 'Improve your mental health – volunteer for a charity.'

A student has started this task. Continue this speech using your own ideas.

- 'Everyone knows that volunteering is a good idea. It has many benefits for both the community and the individual. You just need to find a suitable role and get stuck in.'

> Go for something that suits your interests.

> Makes people feel valuable, gives sense of achievement.

AO5 Development Adding details

You need to add details to each of your ideas to make them effective for your audience. One way to do this is to add examples, explanations or facts such as statistics.

For instance, look at these three paragraphs for a speech about the dangers of using the internet.

❶ One of the dangers of shopping online is that you can easily be taken in by fake selling websites. A friend of mine spent a fortune online buying trainers, only to find out that the site was a scam. The site disappeared and he was never able to reclaim the money.

❶ An example

❷ One of the dangers of using social media sites is that you can never be certain who it is you are speaking to. For instance, older people could be posing as teenagers in chat rooms or on gaming websites. They can strike up a friendship and gain the trust of young people before asking for personal details.

❷ An explanation

❸ One of the dangers of using social media is that it can become addictive. In a recent survey, 75% of teenagers admitted to spending over 3 hours a day online. This time is often at the expense of schoolwork or socialising with friends in the real world.

❸ Facts or statistics

Now **have a go**. Look at this question about recycling. Think of one appropriate idea for a response and write a short paragraph developing your idea with one of the techniques shown above. Use a separate piece of paper for your response.

> Write an online blog post about improving recycling in your local area. You should include:
> - what recycling is happening already
> - what improvements could be made
> - why you think recycling is important.

52

Development Topic sentences

AO5

When answering a writing question, you should start a new paragraph for each of your ideas. Each paragraph should start with a sentence that clearly introduces the idea. This is called a 'topic sentence'.

For instance, look at the start of this paragraph from a speech suggesting all students need to take more exercise.

> ❶ Both my local schools make a big effort to encourage students to take exercise.
>
> ❷ For instance, students are given time at break and lunchtime to join clubs for sports such as football, netball and rounders. One school has also formed a running society which meets weekly in the summer term.

❶ Topic sentence ❷ Two more sentences develop the idea in the topic sentence

Now **have a go**. Add a topic sentence to this paragraph from the same speech about exercise. When you have done that, think of another topic you could include as the next paragraph, and write a topic sentence.

> Teenagers often take the bus to school, use escalators instead of stairs and ask their parents for lifts when they visit friends. The roads near my school are clogged up every day with cars dropping children off and most of them live less than a mile away. If they only walked one way, it would double the amount of exercise they get each day.

A05 Development Building up your ideas

Each of the paragraphs in your answer needs to be fully developed with interesting details. One way to do this is to use adverbial words or phrases to introduce and expand your ideas.

For instance, look at these examples of adverbials you could use in your writing to develop your ideas.

Adding an idea	**Furthermore**, we have no recycling facilities …
	In addition, we need more cycle lanes …
Explaining	**As a result**, pollution is high in the town …
	Therefore, residents are getting ill …
Adding an example	**For example**, the cinema is open all day …
	For instance, the bowling alley is closed on Sundays …
Comparing or contrasting	**Similarly**, the park is often over-crowded …
	However, people do not want …

Now **have a go** at developing another paragraph of a report about town centre facilities. Complete this paragraph by adding appropriate adverbials from the table above. Try not to use the same adverbial more than once. After you have done this, you could write another paragraph using appropriate adverbials to develop your ideas.

> The High Street has a wide variety of facilities to suit all needs and budgets.
>
> _____ it has a small cinema and bowling alley which are both popular with younger residents.
>
> _____ there is not enough parking at present, and _____ the cinema may have to close for part of the week.
>
> Wheelchair users would also like to use these facilities, but they are put off by the poor state of the pavements. _____, they are not able to enjoy a full social life in the town.

_____
_____
_____
_____
_____

Development Signposting

A05

To make your writing effective you should lead your audience through your ideas logically. Once you have decided on the most effective order for your ideas, you can signpost them clearly using adverbials.

For instance, look at these examples of adverbials you could use in your writing to develop your ideas.

Firstly, you could try…

Secondly, I think…

Later I was able to…

Next I found that…

Before we had exams…

Meanwhile, students are suffering…

Finally, I implore you to consider…

Then it became obvious that…

Now **have a go**. Look at this paragraph from a speech with the title 'How to enjoy getting fitter'.

Question 1. Add an appropriate signposting adverbial from the list above.

_____, you should try and find a sport that you actually enjoy. Obviously, it will be harder to get fit and stay fit if you pick an activity only because your friends like it. Perhaps try out a few different sports before deciding which one you like enough to stick to long-term.

Question 2. Write the next paragraph, selecting a suitable adverbial from the table at the start of a clear topic sentence.

AO5 Development Top tips and practice

Top tips:

- Add development details to each of your ideas.
- Use a new paragraph for each of your ideas.
- Use clear topic sentences at the start of each paragraph.
- Use adverbials to develop each of your ideas.
- Signpost your ideas to take your audience clearly through your writing.

Now **have a go**. Read the following question carefully and complete the following tasks. Use a separate piece of paper if you need more space.

- Spend ten minutes writing a plan.
- Add detail to the ideas on your plan; you could add examples, explanations or facts.
- Number your ideas into an effective structure.
- Write **three** paragraphs of an answer, using clear topic sentences and appropriate adverbials to develop your ideas and signpost them clearly for your audience.

> Write a review for a travel website of a place or event you have visited recently.
>
> You should include:
>
> - what is available at the place or event
> - who would enjoy the place or event
> - your opinions about the place or event.

Style Text types

AO5

Your writing needs to be appropriate for purpose. To do this, you need to use the key features of the form you are asked to use.

For instance, look at the start of this answer to a question asking for a review of a place or event.

① Catchy title which often indicates the writer's opinion.

② Engaging opening sentence gives an overview of the writer's experience.

> **①** Planet Pizza – world-beating!
>
> **②** I know some of my readers are convinced that there cannot possibly be anything new in the world of pizzas, but they're wrong. **③** I visited Planet Pizza last week to test their claim that they are literally out of this world. Walking out an hour later (and several pounds heavier) I had to admit that they are right.
>
> **④** From the moment I arrived …

③ The structure is logical to take readers through the whole experience.

④ Further paragraphs add detail.

Now **have a go**. Think about the key features of other types of writing. Draw lines to match the writing types with their appropriate features. Some features match more than one writing type.

Writing types	Appropriate features
Article	Headings
Letter	Headlines
Review	Title
Report	Introduction
Blog	Recommendations
Formal email	Conclusions
Text for a speech	Sub-headings
Section for booklet	Engaging opening paragraph

57

A05 Style Tone

You need to use an appropriate tone (or voice) for your writing, which means thinking carefully about what writing style suits your audience and purpose.

For instance, look at the tone in this paragraph in response to the following question.

> Write an article for your school or college website with the title 'How to combat exam stress'.

> ❶ I know exactly how you're feeling – all around you your mates are smashing it, while you spend your time cowering in your room under a tottering pile of revision cards. If stress means ❷ you're doom scrolling instead of revising, don't panic. Take a breath. I've got your back with some simple tips to get your revision back on track.

❶ Audience of teenage peers, so direct, friendly address is appropriate.

❷ You must avoid slang, but informal words and phrases are appropriate here.

Now **have a go**. Look at the following paragraph about exams written for an article in a national newspaper with the title 'Exam season: How can parents help?'. Underline examples of a formal style that is appropriate for an audience of adults. Note down why you have selected each word or phrase.

> You will already be aware that parents play a vital role in helping their children deal with the stresses and strains of the exam season. You know that your role is to support and encourage, but how exactly do you go about this without causing arguments?

_____
_____
_____
_____
_____
_____

Style Rhetorical devices for emphasis   AO5

To make your writing style engaging and interesting for your reader, you could use rhetorical devices to emphasise your ideas.

For instance, look at these devices and the examples of how they can be used.

❶ You can work hard next year in a job you hate, or you can work hard now and walk into the job of your dreams.

❷ The best toiletries to pack for a hiking trip are those which are small, light, cheap and easily disposable.

❸ Society needs winners. It is the winners in society who get things done.

❶ **Contrast**: putting two opposing ideas in a sentence or paragraph can emphasise the differences between them.

❷ **List**: using a list means you can emphasise a range of ideas in one sentence.

❸ **Repetition**: repeating an idea, word or phrase can make it more memorable.

Now **have a go**. Write one or two paragraphs of an answer to the following question, using each of the rhetorical devices shown above. Use a separate piece of paper if you need more space.

> Write an online review of a product you have purchased recently.
> You should include:
> - what the product is and what it does
> - what you like about the product
> - anything you don't like about the product.

_____
_____
_____
_____
_____
_____
_____

AO5 Style Rhetorical devices for impact

To give your writing impact, particularly if you want to persuade your audience to do something, you could include rhetorical devices.

For instance, look at these devices and the examples of how they can be used:

❶ Would you stand by and watch a friend make a life-changing mistake?

❷ If you don't do something soon, that pile of mouldy plates and festering cups will get up and follow you out of your room.

❸ Recycling is safe, sensible and secure.

❹ New research shows that 75% of teenagers are anxious about their appearance.

❶ **Rhetorical questions:** these can be used to lead your audience to think deeply about your ideas.

❷ **Hyperbole:** this is exaggeration and can add humour or emphasis to your persuasion.

❸ **Alliteration:** this is the repetition of initial letters and adds memorable rhythm to your writing.

❹ **Facts and statistics:** these can make your ideas seem more truthful.

Now **have a go**. Write one or two paragraphs of an answer to the following question, using each of the rhetorical devices shown above. Use a separate piece of paper if you need more space.

> Write an article for your school or college newspaper, encouraging more students to start shopping in charity shops. You should include:
> - what charity shops offer
> - why shopping in charity shops is a good idea
> - your opinions about charity shops.

_____
_____
_____
_____
_____

Style Top tips and practice

Top tips:

- Think about what tone is most appropriate for your audience and purpose.
- If using informal language, avoid slang, abbreviations or text speak.
- Use rhetorical devices to emphasise your ideas.
- Use carefully chosen rhetorical devices if you want to be persuasive.
- Don't overuse devices – make sure they are appropriate to your purpose and audience.

Now **have a go**. Plan and write an answer to the following question, paying particular attention to your tone and using a selection of appropriate rhetorical devices. Use the space around the question to make notes, and a separate piece of paper for your response.

> Write a speech to an audience of your peers putting forward the idea that all 16-year-olds should do a year of community service.
>
> You should include:
>
> - why community service would be a good idea
> - why some might not like community service
> - what your opinions are about community service.

A06

Use a range of vocabulary and sentence structures for clarity, purpose and effect, with accurate spelling and punctuation.

Synonyms

To make your transactional writing effective you need to use varied vocabulary. One way to do this is to use ambitious synonyms (words and phrases that mean the same thing) to avoid over-use of key words.

For instance, look at this question about celebrities, and the student responses. In the second response, the student has improved their first attempt.

> Write an article for a national newspaper with the title 'Celebrities – good role models for the young people of today?'

The ❶idea that ❷celebrities make good role models for young people is wrong. This idea is wrong as celebrities are often not good at stuff and have often done nothing but been on reality TV shows. Celebrities are often only famous for behaving badly or for taking lots of drugs. This can lead to young people getting the wrong idea about what is a good way to live. A good idea is to use sports people as role models.

❶ Over-use of boring vocabulary.

❷ Over-use of key words from question.

The viewpoint that celebrities make good role models for young people is mistaken. This opinion is wrong as they have usually done nothing but appear on reality TV shows. These TV stars are often only famous for behaving badly or for taking lots of drugs. This can lead to teenagers getting dangerous ideas about what is a healthy way to live. A better idea is to use sports men or women as an ideal.

Now **have a go**.

Question 1. Read the second response again – underline the changes that the student has made.

Question 2. On a separate piece of paper, write the next paragraph of a response to the question about celebrities as role models. Avoid over-use of key words in the question and familiar or boring vocabulary.

Vocabulary

AO6

To make your transactional writing effective you need to use varied vocabulary. One way to do this is to think of the connotations (hidden meanings) of your vocabulary choices.

For instance, look at the first two sentences of a student response to the question below. Then look at the alternative word choices that they could have used in each sentence.

> Write a letter to the Head of your school or college about a proposal to make homework compulsory.

> Forcing teenagers to add two or three more hours of work on to a long school day will just leave them ❶tired.
>
> Making homework compulsory is a ❷horrible way to treat young people.

❶
exhausted – suggests extreme tiredness
sleepy – sounds childish
drained – suggests weakness

❷
brutal – suggests violent, very harsh
shocking – suggests something surprising
callous – suggests cruel lack of feeling

Now **have a go**.

Question 1. Select the most appropriate alternative word choice given for each of the sentences above. Write a sentence explaining your choices.

Alternative to 'tired': _____

_____

Alternative to 'horrible': _____

_____

Question 2. Think of three alternatives to the word 'compulsory'. Circle the best of the three and write a sentence explaining your choice.

Alternatives to 'compulsory': _____

_____

_____

AO6 Sentence openings

One way to add impact to your transactional writing is to pay close attention to the way you open your sentences. Using a variety of different sentences will make your ideas more engaging for your readers.

For instance, look at these different ways to start a sentence about following fashion.

1. We all become like sheep …
2. Between the fashion magazines and the Instagram influencers …
3. Buying everything we see on social media …
4. Huge amounts of clothes are sent to landfill …
5. Surprisingly, many young people are turning away from fast fashion …

1. **A pronoun:** I, you, he, she, it, we, they, my, your, his, her, their

2. **A preposition (a word that tells you the position of something or someone):** above, behind, between, near, with, on, under

3. **An '-ing' verb:** running, hurrying, waiting, holding

4. **An adjective (a describing word):** slow, quiet, large, huge

5. **An adverb (a word that describes a verb):** unfortunately, painfully, happily, quickly

Now **have a go**. Using the examples above as a model, write two paragraphs in response to the following question. Try to avoid using 'the' or 'a' more than once at the start of your sentences.

> Write a speech for an audience of your peers with the title 'The dangers of fast fashion'.

Sentence style and punctuation   AO6

To make your transactional writing effective, you need to use a variety of sentence structures and punctuate them appropriately.

For instance, look at the sentence variety and punctuation used in this paragraph about the importance of education.

❶ Short sentences can add emphasis at the start or end of a paragraph.

❷ Commas can be used to separate items in a list.

> ❶Education changes lives. It helps people gain ❷knowledge, develop skills, gain confidence and build a better future. Secondary ❸schools, where we study a variety of subjects, help us to decide what path we want to take in life. It was my English ❹teacher – Mrs Lee – who gave me my love of English and made me want to become a writer.

❸ Commas can be used to add extra explanations to your sentences.

❹ Dashes can be used to add emphasis to extra information.

Now **have a go**. Using the paragraph above as a model, write another paragraph in response to the following question about education. Use a separate piece of paper if you need more space.

> Write a speech for your peers with the title 'Education changes lives'.

AO6 Top tips and practice

Top tips:

- Use synonyms to avoid repeating key words in the question.
- Think about the connotations of your vocabulary choices.
- Use a variety of different sentence openings.
- Use punctuation to create a variety of sentence styles.
- Always end your sentence with the appropriate punctuation.
- Before you use an exclamation mark, ask yourself if it is appropriate to your audience and purpose.

Now **have a go**. Write a full answer to the following question, paying particular attention to your vocabulary, sentence style and punctuation.

Before you start your response, spend **10** minutes using the space around the question to write a plan. Use a separate piece of paper for your response.

> Write a letter to your local Council giving your views about a plan to build a skateboard ramp at your local park.
>
> You should include:
>
> - ideas about why it is a good idea
> - ideas about why it might be a bad idea
> - your views about the plan.

A05 Communicate clearly, effectively and imaginatively, selecting and adapting tone, style and register for different forms, purposes and audience.

Imaginative writing | Plan Selecting a question

A05 **Imaginative writing** questions appear on Paper 2. First, you need to select your question carefully from a choice of two. The purpose of the writing is to entertain, and you should make your writing engaging enough to appeal to a wide audience.

For instance, have a look at the annotations for the questions below.

❶ Imaginative: the writing should be original and creative, using an interesting plot and characters that your reader care about.

> Write an ❶ imaginative piece that starts with the line:
>
> '❷ I knew ❸ the minute I saw them that we would all be friends for life.'

❷ Narrative voice: it is probably easier to continue this type of response in the first person.

❸ Opening line: this gives an idea of theme and helps to generate ideas.

❹ Narrative voice: you can write in first or third person.

❺ Real or imagined: you can write about something that has happened or make something up.

> Write about a time ❹ you, or someone you know, met someone new.
>
> Your response could be ❺ real or imagined.
>
> You may wish to base your response on ❻ one of the images provided or use any ideas of your own.

❻ Images: two images will be provided on the exam paper, you can use them as prompts for ideas, but you should still use a clear structure rather than just doing a description.

Now **have a go**.

Circle the best way to approach an imaginative writing question.

| Select the question you can write the most about. | Select the question that you can answer with originality. | Use a story you have written before. |

67

AO5 Plan Gathering ideas

Before starting your answer to an imaginative writing question, you should spend around **10** minutes planning. One way to gather ideas during the planning stage is to think about the question you have chosen and write down everything that comes into your mind. This is called 'thought association'.

For instance, look at this question about a celebration. The student has gathered ideas about celebrating a sporting win.

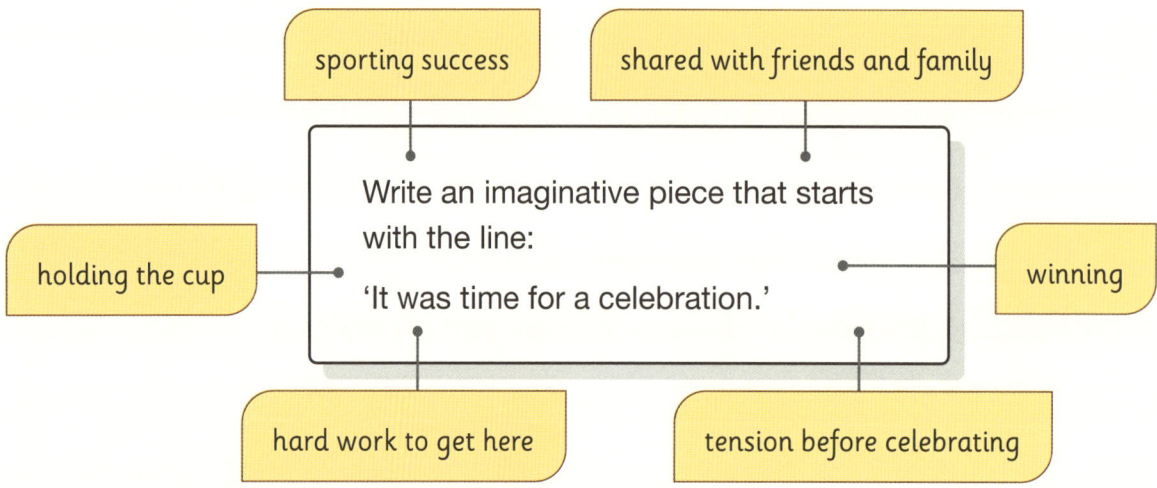

Now **have a go** at using thought association for the following question about friendship. Use a separate piece of paper if you need more space.

> Write about a time you, or someone you know, found something hidden.

Plan Using an image

A05

One of the questions will have images that you can use as a prompt for your writing. You can use this as a prompt when you are planning. One way to do this is to ask 'who', 'what', 'why' and 'where' questions.

For instance, look at the student's annotations on the image below for a question about a journey.

What is happening? Stuck in snow, not moved for hours

Who is there? My family – younger brother, Mum and Step-dad.

Write about a time you, or someone you know, went on a long journey.

Where are we going? On way to new house in new city.

Why are we there? Have to move for mum's new job.

Now **have a go**. Look at the question above and come up with your own answers to the 'who', 'what', 'why' and 'where' questions.

Who?
_____
_____

Where?
_____
_____

Why?
_____
_____

What?
_____
_____

A05 Plan Three-part story plan

During your **10 minute's** planning time you could gather ideas in a three-part story plan.

For instance, look at the question about telling a lie. Notice that the question is simple, with just one main event and only a few characters. Then look at the student's plan – it includes the exposition, climax, and resolution.

> Write an imaginative piece that starts with the line:
>
> 'It seemed like such a small lie.'

❶ Exposition	Enter guitar competition to impress friends but can't really play.
❷ Climax	Secretly practise for hours and hours, friends tell whole school how good I am, I panic about competition and stop seeing friends.
❸ Resolution	Day of concert arrives, friends turn up laughing as they knew all along I couldn't play. I surprise them with perfect song.

❶ Beginning of story, setting of scene and introduction of characters.

❷ Main action, the high point of the story.

❸ Ending, which can be happy or sad.

Now **have a go**. Come up with your own ideas for the question about telling a lie.

Exposition

Climax

Resolution

Plan Top tips and practice — AO5

Top tips:

- Select a question that you can answer with originality and creativity.
- Spend **10** minutes gathering ideas before you start your answer.
- Use one of the following planning methods:
  - thought association
  - 'what', 'why', 'where' and 'when' questions
  - a three-part story plan.
- Keep it simple – one main event and just a couple of characters.

Now **have a go** at gathering ideas for the following question.

Use a separate piece of paper if you need more space.

> Write an imaginative piece that starts with the line:
>
> 'I knew from the start that it was a really bad idea.'

A05 Structure Structuring for effect

As part of your planning process, you need to consider the structure of your narrative. One way to start is with the narrative voice – that is the viewpoint from which you want to tell the story.

For instance, look at the following question and the two different narrative viewpoints that could be used in a response.

> Write about a time when you, or someone you know, faced a frightening situation.

1 I dug my heels tighter into the stirrups, clung desperately to the reins and prayed that the ride would end soon. This was going to be one birthday surprise I would never forget.

1 **First person** narration using the pronoun 'I': this encourages a reader to sympathise with the narrator's actions and feelings.

2 The boy clung tightly to the animal's back as his father looked on anxiously from a distance. Both were desperately praying that the ride would end soon, and without serious injury.

2 **Third person** narration using the pronouns 'he' or 'she': the narrator is not a character in the story which means the reader can be told the thoughts and feelings of every character.

Now **have a go**. Look again at the question about a frightening situation and write your own paragraphs using two different narrative voices.

First person: _____
_____
_____
_____

Third person: _____
_____
_____
_____

Structure Flashback

A05

One way to structure your narrative is by using a chronological approach and starting at the beginning. Another way is to start with the main event and then work back to the exposition or beginning – this is called a 'flashback'.

For instance, look at these two plans for a response to a question about a mysterious visitor. Each one uses a different order to tell the events.

	Chronological structure	Flashback structure
Exposition	Two friends home alone on a dark stormy night.	Knock on door, nobody there.
Climax	Knock on door, nobody there, one friend goes out to look.	Two friends home alone on a dark stormy night. One friend goes out to investigate.
Resolution	Friend never comes back, mystery remains unsolved. Narrator never stays home alone again.	Narrator waits but friend never comes back. Narrator never stays home alone again.

Now **have a go**. Make your own chronological plan for a question about a mysterious visitor. Then see if it works better using a 'flashback' structure.

	Chronological structure	Flashback structure
Exposition		
Climax		
Resolution		

AO5 Structure Openings

You should always think carefully about how to engage your readers from the start of your writing. Your opening should entertain your reader enough to make them read on to the end. There are several different ways to do this.

For instance, look at the following ways to start a response to a question about telling a lie.

1 At the time, it seemed like such a little lie. But everything that's happened since then means it now seems much, much bigger.

1 With a mystery

2 Crash! The ball arced through the air and smashed through the window.

2 With action

3 I heard his footsteps before I saw him. After all these years he was here. My lie was finally going to catch up with me.

3 With danger or conflict

Now **have a go**. Using the above examples as a model, write your own three openings to a question about telling a lie.

With a mystery: _____
_____
_____
_____

With action: _____
_____
_____
_____

With danger or conflict: _____
_____
_____
_____

Structure Endings   A05

You should always think carefully about how to end your writing. The ending is the final impression the reader has of your writing, so it needs to have impact.

For instance, look at these three ways to end a response about making a serious mistake.

❶ Later, everybody wondered what all the fuss had been about. Nobody was hurt, nobody had died. He clutched his sister's hand tightly and walked away.

❶ Resolution of conflict

❷ Suddenly I knew what I had to do. I was going to stand up for myself once and for all. I needed to tell the truth.

❷ Cliffhanger

❸ She looked up at him and smiled. The pain of the last twenty years melted away as he realised that waiting for her hadn't been a mistake after all.

❸ A twist

Now **have a go**. Using the above examples as a model, write your own three endings to a question about making a serious mistake.

Resolution of conflict: _____

_____

_____

Cliffhanger: _____

_____

_____

A twist: _____

_____

_____

A05 Structure Top tips and practice

Top tips:

- Think carefully about what narrative voice you want to use.
- Structure your narrative carefully, starting with an engaging part from your plan.
- Use an engaging technique to open your writing.
- Make sure your ending leaves a lasting impression on your reader.

Now **have a go**. Look at the question below, and a student's three-part plan. Then follow the list of prompts to develop an answer to the question. Use a separate piece of paper for your response.

> Write an imaginative piece that starts with the line:
>
> 'It was well hidden.'

1 Bored on a beach holiday with family, find a bottle on beach with a message inside.

1 Exposition

2 Message reads 'help me'.

Contact police and rescue services, newspaper prints story – get famous on social media.

2 Climax

3 After six weeks younger brother admits to putting bottle on sand, feel foolish when news gets out.

3 Resolution

- Decide which structure to use: chronological starting with exposition, or flashback.
- Renumber the three parts of the student's plan **1–3**, so that **1** is the part you would use as the opening.
- Decide which narrative voice to use.
- Choose the most appropriate opening technique and write the opening paragraph.
- Choose a technique for the ending which will have lasting impact. Write the ending using the technique you have chosen.

Development Adding details to your plan

A05

When you are planning your imaginative writing, you need to think about how to add detail. To make it engaging, avoid explaining every small detail and focus on the most interesting parts of your plan.

For instance, look at the detail added to this plan for a response to a question about trying hard at something. Notice that the plan is simple, but the added details will ensure the response is engaging for a reader.

Three-part plan	Development
Exposition: Enter first marathon	Feelings of excitement Punishing training schedule No previous experience
Climax: Fall at half-way point	Get blisters early in race Stumble over loose paving stone Limp for several miles
Resolution: Get to finish line?	See friends in crowd Make final effort Finish or not?

Now **have a go**. Look at another plan for a question about trying hard at something. Add details that will make the response engaging. One has been added for you.

Exposition: I decide to try hard to be nicer to my younger brother	
Climax: younger brother lets his pet snake lose in my room	Snake silent under bed
Resolution: I take revenge	

77

A05 Development Character creation

To make your writing engaging you need to create believable characters. One way to make them interesting is to 'show' readers what they are like, rather than 'telling'.

For instance, look at these two examples about a character called Naima who kicks a football through a classroom window.

1 Naima loved football, was the star of the school team and practised as many hours as she could. She was so tall that she headed the ball straight over the desks and out of the window. She loved it when everyone in the class clapped.

1 **Tell:** Readers are told exactly what Naima is like.

2 Naima's head nearly hit the ceiling when she headed the ball. It sailed over the desks and smashed through the classroom window. She grinned as she heard the applause of her classmates. All those hours practising with the school team had been worth it.

2 **Show:** Readers are shown what Naima is like through her actions; it is her grin that suggests she is enjoying the applause.

Now **have a go**. Read this short paragraph about a character called Jamal who gives the narrator some bad news. Re-write it using the 'show not tell' technique.

> Jamal was a small and quiet boy who was happiest sitting in his room playing computer games. He was very excited to share his new game with his best friend Ray. Ray loved it when he beat Jamal the first time they played the game together.

Development Settings   A05

Imaginative writing needs believable settings. You can use the 'show not tell' technique to make your settings more interesting for your readers.

For instance, look at these short paragraphs about accepting a dare.

❶ My friends chose the tallest old tree in the park for my dare. I could see the wind blowing its branches as I looked up. My knees knocked as I walked towards it.

❶ Tell: Readers are told the tree is tall and old, and that the wind is blowing.

❷ The tree my friends chose for me had always loomed over the others in the small wood at the side of our local park. I had to crane my neck to see where its swaying branches reached high into the gathering clouds. My knees knocked as I walked towards it.

❷ Show: Readers are shown that the tree is old, and vivid description is used to help readers picture the scene.

Now **have a go**. Use the 'show not tell' technique to create your own believable and interesting setting for a question about accepting a dare.

_____
_____
_____
_____
_____
_____
_____
_____
_____
_____
_____
_____

A05 — Development Paragraphs

Your imaginative writing needs to be developed into paragraphs to make it easier for readers to follow your ideas.

For instance, it is a good idea to start a new paragraph when:

- ❶ you move forwards or backwards in time
- ❷ you move to a new setting
- ❸ you introduce a new character, or a new plot development.

For example:

> ❶ **Later**, Ben settled back in his chair in front of the fire. It had been a long and frustrating day and all he could think about was soothing his aching back.
>
> ❷ **Outside**, rain lashed against the windows and wind whistled loudly through the trees. Leaves danced around the garden and skidded across the surface of the freezing pond. The night was closing in.
>
> ❸ **The doorbell rang** and Ben sighed. He was just beginning to feel comfortable and had no great desire for company. Groaning softly, he stood, put on his slippers and made his way towards the front door.

Now **have a go**. Write the next two paragraphs to this response, which is about the arrival of a mysterious stranger. One should introduce a new character, and the other should move forward in time.

Development Top tips and practice

AO5

Top tips:
- Add development details to each of your ideas when planning.
- Create interesting characters using the 'show not tell' technique.
- Create interesting settings by using the 'show not tell' technique.
- Use paragraphs to make it easier for your reader to follow your ideas.

Now **have a go**. Read the following question carefully. Then follow the prompts to develop an answer. Use a separate piece of paper if you need more space.

> Write an imaginative piece with the opening line:
>
> 'It was a wonderful opportunity.'

- Plan a simple three-part narrative.
- Add details to make the most interesting parts of your plan.
- Write one paragraph about the main character, using the 'show not tell' technique.
- Write the next paragraph, moving the action forward or changing the setting.

AO5 Style Tone

When planning your imaginative writing you should always consider how you want your readers to feel. One way to approach this is to consider what **tone** (or mood) you want to create.

For instance, look at these opening paragraphs to a question with the opening line 'I remember the day as if it were yesterday'. Language techniques have been carefully chosen to create different tones for the reader.

❶ I remember the day as if it were yesterday. My pounding heart, the sweat breaking out on my forehead. I inched forwards carefully, never taking my eyes off it for a second. If I could just get to the door, I could call for help.

The snake hissed…

❶ A **tense tone** is built up by creating vivid images of the narrator's fear before revealing what he is frightened of.

❷ I remember the day as if it were yesterday. The ocean glistened like a rare jewel in the distance. A gentle breeze rustled the bushes beside my chair. The champagne cooled invitingly in a silver ice bucket. It was going to be the greatest proposal in history.

❷ Metaphor and vivid imagery are used to create a **romantic tone**.

❸ I remember the day as if it were yesterday. As I opened the door it was the smell that reached me first, a cross between hundreds of pairs of my brother's dirty socks, and a yoghurt several years past its sell by date.

❸ A **humorous tone** is created through using sensory images.

Now **have a go**. Using one of the paragraphs above as a model, write an opening paragraph to a question about helping a friend. Use a separate piece of paper if you need more space.

_____
_____
_____

Style Metaphors and similes

AO5

You can make your writing more engaging by creating powerful images in your readers' minds. One way to do this is to use metaphors or similes.

For instance, look at the way metaphors and similes have been used in these extracts from a question about a day at the seaside.

> The sea glistened ❶ like a rare blue jewel and the sun beat down upon miles of pristine yellow sand. It was already hot at nine am and I knew the beach ❷ would be a furnace by midday.
>
> It was war. Armies of people defended their patch of sand with towels and beach umbrellas. Seagulls swooped like vultures, pouncing on anything that looked like food.

❶ Similes use the words 'as' or 'like' to help readers visualise the scene.

❷ Metaphors are direct comparisons and create vivid images.

Now **have a go**. Read the following question and think about what images you want to create for a reader.

> Write about a time when you, or someone you know, met a hero.

Now write a few similes and metaphors of your own. Try to avoid obvious metaphors that your reader will have heard many times before (such as: cool as a cucumber, white as a sheet, brave as a lion).

Metaphors:

_____

_____

_____

Similes:

_____

_____

_____

AO5 Style Figurative language

You can make your writing engaging and interesting by using figurative language techniques such as **personification**, **hyperbole** and **alliteration**. These techniques can create images in the reader's mind, helping them to imagine your setting or characters.

You can use a combination of techniques in one sentence to emphasise an image. But be careful not to overdo it; they must all work together.

For instance, look at these extracts from a question about being lost.

> **1** A thick fog crept silently from the trees, seeping in through the car windows and settling like thick soup around our faces.

1 Personification: giving human actions to something non-human can create tension or humour.

> **2** The cold was so intense I feared becoming an ice statue.

2 Hyperbole: exaggeration can create humour or a vivid image.

> **3** Sunlight streamed through the trees, their shadows gently dancing in the cool evening breeze.

3 Alliteration: this can add interesting rhythm to your writing.

Now have a go. Write your own three sentences about being lost, using a combination of the techniques above. Try to stick to one overall image in each of your sentences.

_____
_____
_____
_____
_____
_____
_____
_____
_____

Style Using the senses

AO5

You can develop your imaginative ideas and create effects by using the five senses to 'show' rather than 'tell' your reader what your characters are feeling. Using the five senses and thinking about what characters can see, hear, feel, smell and taste, helps your readers to picture the scene.

For instance, look at the two examples in response to a question about finding something unpleasant. The first just 'tells' readers what is happening, while the second uses the senses to 'show'.

> The fridge was ❶crammed to bursting with mouldy, stinking food that was way past its sell by date. There was what looked like a block of cheese festering at the back and something soft and furry hiding behind it. Surely there wasn't an actual mouse in the fridge?

❶ This has some descriptive vocabulary, but 'tells' readers exactly what is in the fridge.

> As soon as he opened the fridge door the smell of rotting food ❷assaulted his nostrils. Peering cautiously into its depths his eyes landed on a festering block of cheese. Reaching out his fingers he brushed against something soft and furry. It squeaked. Surely there wasn't an actual mouse in the fridge?

❷ Careful use of the senses improves the description by 'showing' readers what the character is feeling, seeing, smelling and hearing.

Now **have a go**. Imagine a character has found something unpleasant under the bed. Write a sentence of description using each of the five senses.

Sight: _____

Smell: _____

Touch: _____

Taste: _____

Sound: _____

AO5 Style Top tips and practice

Top tips:

- Think about what tone or mood is most appropriate for your ideas.
- Use metaphors or similes that are appropriate for your ideas.
- Use figurative language such as personification to create vivid images for your readers.
- Use the five senses to make your descriptions more interesting.
- Don't overuse figurative language or use metaphors that are too obvious.

Now **have a go**. Plan and write an answer to the following question, paying particular attention to your tone and using a selection of appropriate figurative language. Use the space around the question for your plan, and a separate piece of paper for your response.

> Write about a time you, or someone you know, visited a friend in another town.

A06
Use a range of vocabulary and sentence structures for clarity, purpose and effect, with accurate spelling and punctuation.

Vocabulary

To make your imaginative writing effective you need to use varied vocabulary. Your choices will need to be appropriate for the voice you have selected for your response. One way to do this is to think of the connotations (hidden meanings) of your vocabulary choices.

For instance, a good place to start is with your choice of verbs, adverbs and adjectives.

Look at the different options for the following sentences describing a day trip. In the first paragraph it seems as if Stella is excited to get on the bus, but in the second she seems to be put off by the noisy children.

> Stella ❶ jogged towards the bus. She could ❷ already make out through the windows that it was full of ❸ excited children, chatting animatedly and munching on big bags of crisps.

❶ verbs

> Stella ❶ dawdled towards the bus. She could ❷ already glimpse through the windows that it was full of ❸ boisterous children, shouting loudly and scoffing monster sized bags of crisps.

❷ verbs with adverbs

❸ adjectives

Now **have a go**. Read the next sentence about Stella on the bus. Re-write it, changing the underlined verbs and adverbs so that it seems as if Stella is about to enjoy the bus ride. Then add another sentence or two using your own ideas and appropriate vocabulary choices.

> After <u>walking</u> <u>cautiously</u> down the centre aisle, Stella <u>carefully</u> <u>chose</u> an empty seat next to a window.

_____
_____
_____
_____

AO6 Imagery

One way to add impact to your imaginative writing is to focus on details that create a vivid image for your readers. You can do this by avoiding obvious descriptive words and using the 'show not tell' technique instead.

For instance, look at the differences in the words and phrases used to describe characters and settings in the following sentences. The examples in the 'Show' column use the 'show not tell' method to improve the vocabulary of the examples in the 'Tell' column.

Tell	Show
I looked down at his old shoes…	I looked down at his scuffed, stained trainers…
Her blonde hair shone in the sunlight…	Her golden locks shone in the sunlight…
The old house was on the outskirts of town, its windows dark and its paint peeling.	The house sat on the very edge of town, its windows blank and lifeless, and its paint flaking away in the wind.
The weather was bad, with heavy rain and strong winds blowing leaves across the garden.	Rain pounded relentlessly against the windows, while gusts of wind bent branches and scattered leaves across the garden.

Now **have a go**. First underline the changes made in the sentences in the 'Show' column above. Then use the 'show not tell' method to improve the vocabulary in the following boring descriptions. Concentrate on using words or phrases that create strong images for a reader.

Tell	Show
The man was tall and dark haired.	
The girl wore an old, worn coat.	
Sun shone out of the clean windows.	
It was a stormy winter day.	

Sentence openings   A06

Another way to add impact to your imaginative writing is to pay close attention to the way you open your sentences. Using a variety of different sentences will make your ideas more engaging for your readers.

For instance, look at these different ways to start a sentence.

❶ I turned and stared …

❷ Behind me was a large cheering crowd …

❸ Edging silently towards the door …

❹ Sharp prickling feelings of fear …

❺ Gingerly, I peered out into the darkness …

❶ **A pronoun:** I, you, he, she, it, we, they, my, your, his, her, their

❷ **A preposition (a word that tells you the position of something or someone):** above, behind, between, near, with, on, under

❸ **An '-ing' verb:** running, hurrying, waiting, holding

❹ **An adjective (a describing word):** slow, quiet, large, huge

❺ **An adverb (a word that describes a verb):** unfortunately, painfully, happily, quickly

Now **have a go**. Using the examples above as a model, write **two** paragraphs in response to the question below. Try to avoid using 'the' or 'a' more than once at the start of your sentences. Use a separate piece of paper if you need more space.

Write an imaginative piece that starts with the line:

'It all started so well.'

_____

_____

_____

_____

_____

_____

_____

AO6 — Sentence style and punctuation

To make your imaginative writing effective, you need to use a variety of sentence structures and punctuation.

For instance, look at the sentence variety and punctuation used in this paragraph about an unexpected visitor.

1 Use commas to add extra explanations to your sentences.

2 Use commas to separate items in a list.

3 Use dashes to add emphasis to extra information.

> We sat inside that **¹room, in the dark**, for seven hours. After an hour or so the fire died, and our teeth began to chatter. I was **²cold, hungry, tired** and very frightened. My sister **³Sarah – a very nervous child –** started to whimper like a wounded animal, tears streaking down her face. **⁴Then we heard a bang.**
>
> '**⁵He's back!**' gasped Sarah, grabbing my hand tightly.

4 Short sentences can create tension at the start or end of a paragraph.

5 Use exclamation marks to add tension or humour. Dialogue should be clearly contained within speech marks.

Now **have a go**. Using the paragraph above as a model, write another paragraph in response to the following question. Use a separate piece of paper if you need more space.

> Write about a time you, or someone you know, had an unexpected visitor.

Proof reading

AO6

It is essential that you leave time at the end of your writing to check your grammar – this means proofreading your response to check it makes sense.

For instance, this paragraph contains several common types of errors made in imaginative writing responses.

① Spelling mistakes: think carefully whether letters need doubling, and whether the word starts with a silent letter.

② Apostrophes: always needed for possession and omission.

③ Punctuation: full stops and capital letters must be used. Speech marks are needed for dialogue.

This was my moment. This is when I ①finaly proove that I can do it.

I think back to my ②mothers words this morning, ③④Your fine she ⑤says before I left for school. ③It doesnt matter if you get it rong.

In front of me swam row upon row of eager faces, there eyes all sparkling with excitement. my heart pounds and my palms sweat as I inhaled deeply and pulled back my shoulders. Silence slowly creept threw the huge hall and the air becomes very still. Nothing happened. I freeze in fear.

---

④ Homophones: some words sound the same but are spelt differently. Learn commonly used homophones such as 'their/there/they're' and 'your/you're'.

⑤ Tense: it is best to use the same tense throughout your writing.

Now **have a go**. The paragraph above was written in response to this imaginative writing question.

> Write about a time when you, or someone you know, had to perform in front of a crowd of people.

Re-write the paragraph, correcting all the errors. Then write the next paragraph of the response. Proofread your paragraph carefully and correct any errors. Use a separate piece of paper if you need more space.

_____
_____
_____
_____

A06 Top tips and practice

Top tips:

- Think about the connotations of your vocabulary choices.
- Use the 'show not tell' technique to add imagery to your writing.
- Use punctuation to create a variety of sentence styles.
- Always end your sentence with appropriate punctuation and be sparing with exclamation marks.
- Avoid too much dialogue and always use speech marks.
- Always proofread your work for errors.

Now **have a go**. Write a full answer to the following exam style question, paying particular attention to your vocabulary, sentence style and punctuation.

Before you start your response, spend **10** minutes using the space around the question to write a plan. Use a separate piece of paper for your response.

When you have finished, spend **5** minutes proofreading your work.

Write about a time you, or someone you know, felt under pressure.

Your response could be real or imagined.

You may wish to base your response on one of the images provided or use any ideas of your own.

Full reading texts

Text A 19th century

This letter was written to a newspaper expressing the writer's support for a decision to allow people to wash in the River Serpentine.

Bathing in the River

1 Sir, – I read in your paper of this morning a querulous letter from a "Constant Reader" respecting the numbers of poor people who are,
5 I am happy to find, now permitted to bathe in the Serpentine River. I wonder that you, who so lately employed your pen in showing the necessity of providing the means
10 of general ablution[1] for the bodies of our poor working people, should now publish the complaints of this person. What are the poor people to do? There are no free baths provided by the State; the great highway of the Thames is
15 interdicted[2], perhaps not improperly; but with respect to the Serpentine River, there can be no objection to the use of it as a great public bath.

If "constant readers" and others of such sickly fancies do not like to witness the scene of so much enjoyment, let them go somewhere else and take their "quiet walks", for the walkers, quiet or otherwise, may go to many places, whereas the bathers can go to but
20 this one. For my part, I cannot sufficiently express my gratitude to those in authority who have had the merciful kindness to allow the poor working man to refresh and strengthen his body in the comfort and salubrity[3] of a bath in the Serpentine River.

1 Ablution – washing
2 Interdicted – forbidden
3 Salubrity – good for your health

Full reading texts

Text B   19th century

In this extract from a girl's magazine article of 1880, the writer gives advice about how to swim in the sea safely.

Baths by the Sea

1   And now for a word by the sad sea wave. A course of sea-bathing, even if it only lasts for a week or a fortnight, and if taken judiciously, is extremely invigorating. The first thing that most young girls do when they first go to the seaside is to "go wild." You will pardon me the expression, I am <u>sure</u>; it is meant for your good, and to warn you <u>against</u> that
5   over-excitement which the very sight of the ocean hardly ever fails to induce in the young. This ought to be kept within bounds; pleasure to be obtained at the seaside, if it is to be beneficial, ought to be more of the quiet and dreamy kind. While feeling thus you are laying up a store of health and vigour which will do you excellent service when you get back to town or to your own inland home.

10 I do not advise any girl to begin bathing the very first day of her arrival at the seaside. Better she should spend this day loitering on the sands or among the rocks, where, if she has any taste for the beautiful, she will find a thousand and one objects to interest her. Indeed, at the seaside one cannot be too much out of doors, and as for children they may with benefit paddle about among the wavelets, or build sand castles all day long. Avoid
15 parties and concerts while on your maritime[1] holiday. Your pleasures ought to be of the very quietest nature possible.

Take plenty of exercise, but do not fatigue yourself, and beware of a too hot sun. Go to bed early and be up before the mists of morning have quite gathered themselves off the sea. Do not forget that the evenings are often chilly; it is well, therefore, if you mean
20 to enjoy a walk after nightfall, to change your dress for it, putting on thicker boots, and flannels[2] ought always to be worn, for the changes of temperature are often very trying even to the robust.

While at the seaside you ought to enjoy yourself all you can. I only want to warn you against excitement and fatigue.

25 Now as to actual sea-bathing. If you are really strong and hardy you may have a dip in the ocean before breakfast; in most cases, however, it is far better to wait until the day is more advanced – about three hours after the morning meal would therefore be the best time. Do not hurry down to the seaside, but walk at a moderately brisk rate, so that you may be neither very hot nor too cold. Nothing is more dangerous than going into the water either
30 fatigued or cold.

---

1   Maritime – seaside
2   Flannels – a type of linen trousers

Full reading texts

Text C   19th century

In this extract from a 19th century article, the writer describes his first experience of travelling on the London underground.

Memories of London

1 I went down two or three staircases to find myself all of a sudden transported from broad daylight to the middle of the night; flickering
5 lights, people, noise, trains arriving and disappearing out of and into the dark. My train comes in and stops; its passengers hurry out and those waiting jump into the carriages. As
10 I try to work out where the second-class[1] compartments are, the train leaves. "What's happening? Doesn't it stop?!" I asked one of the station staff. "Don't you worry, sir, here's
15 another one coming in." The trains don't just arrive one after the other, they seem to be pursuing each other. It comes in, I jump aboard, and off it moves, as swift as an arrow. A new spectacle begins. We run between the foundations of the city, deep in the unknown. First we descend into an impenetrable darkness, followed by a brief glimpse of feeble daylight; then back into the dark, interrupted every now and then by strange flashes
20 of light; then we emerge into a station lit by hundreds of lamps, only for the station to disappear after a moment. Other trains pass by, but you can't see them. There's a sudden stop at a station, with the thousand faces of the waiting crowd lit up as if by a great fire; and then off we go again, with a deafening noise of doors being slammed shut, bells being rung, machinery grunting; again darkness, more trains passing by, more glimpses of
25 daylight, more illuminated stations, more crowds of people passing, arriving, leaving, until we reach the terminus[2].

---

1 Second-class – the second best type of seat on the train
2 Terminus – the place where the journey ends

Full reading texts

Text D 19th century

In this extract from an 1860 magazine article, the writer hopes that leaving long hair loose and flowing will become fashionable.

Flowing Hair for Ladies

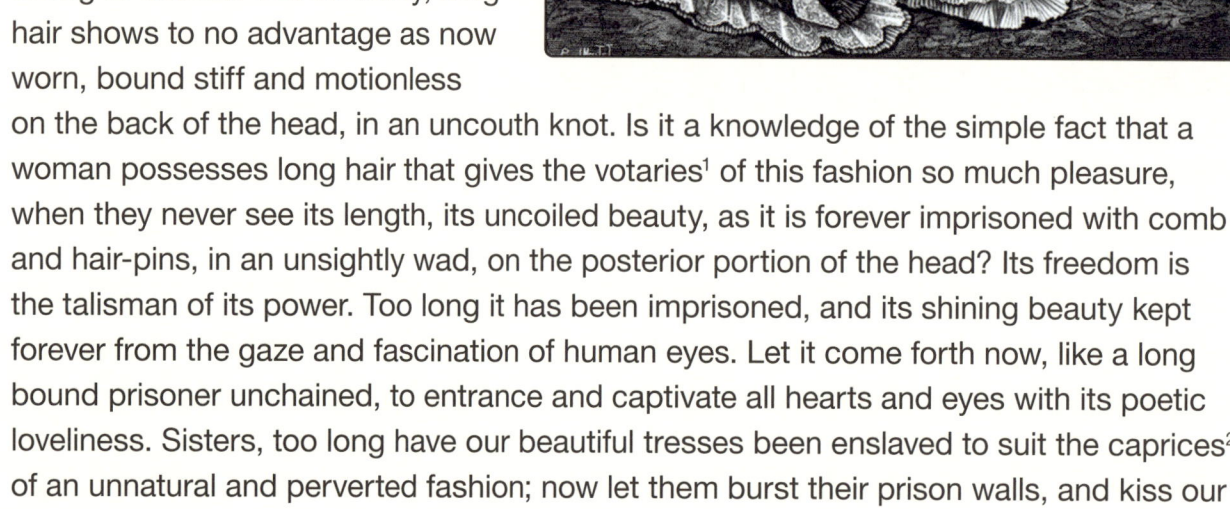

1 I have ever been an admirer of flowing or short hair for ladies, and have been hoping, for several years, that some of the fashion-
5 starting ladies would start this fashion. I know it is contended by many that long hair best becomes a woman. This is, doubtless, true, if worn naturally, as was originally
10 intended, falling gracefully over the neck and shoulders; but, worn in this way, its length becomes an inconvenience that few of us seem willing to endure. But certainly, long
15 hair shows to no advantage as now worn, bound stiff and motionless on the back of the head, in an uncouth knot. Is it a knowledge of the simple fact that a woman possesses long hair that gives the votaries[1] of this fashion so much pleasure, when they never see its length, its uncoiled beauty, as it is forever imprisoned with comb
20 and hair-pins, in an unsightly wad, on the posterior portion of the head? Its freedom is the talisman of its power. Too long it has been imprisoned, and its shining beauty kept forever from the gaze and fascination of human eyes. Let it come forth now, like a long bound prisoner unchained, to entrance and captivate all hearts and eyes with its poetic loveliness. Sisters, too long have our beautiful tresses been enslaved to suit the caprices[2]
25 of an unnatural and perverted fashion; now let them burst their prison walls, and kiss our temples freely, as they are wont to do, and float at will upon the breath of every passing, sylph[3]-winged zephyr[4].

---

1 Votaries – people who like something
2 Caprices – impulses
3 Sylph – imaginary spirit
4 Zephyr – a soft breeze

Full reading texts

Text E 19th century

In this extract from a newspaper article of 1874, the writer describes the advantages of growing a moustache.

The Moustache

1   A moustache makes itself evident at once, unless it be of that pale yellow kind which requires the observer to use a microscope in order to detect it. Brains are not supposed to be visible, and indications of them are not always surface indications.

Formerly, black moustaches were considered the thing. All the heroes of all the novels
5   had them. Fierce, black moustaches: and whenever it became necessary in the course of events to mention the fact that the hero kissed the heroine, it was expressly stated that "his moustached lip touched her downy cheek," etc. etc. This statement was to assure the reader that he did not shave his moustache off before the honeyed operation.

But now – behold! We change all that! Novelists of today have done with black
10 moustaches – they have changed their colours.

Blonde moustaches are all the go with novelists. So young men, if you desire to be in style, raise a tawny[1] moustache. Let it grow long, so that your mouth will be submerged – so that nobody will know for certain that you have got a mouth. It will learn lookers on a lesson of faith in things unseen.

15 To our mind there is no more delicate and affecting sight than to behold a manly youth, with a noble soul in his breast, and a tawny moustache on his lip, gallantly striving to eat tapioca pudding[2] with maple sirup for sauce and not leave the traces of vanished sweetness on his moustache. At the public tables we have watched these determined spirits with eager interest, with sympathy swelling our heart, and tears of admiration in our
20 eyes.

There is another and incalculable advantage in a moustache. It gives a young man employment to stroke it. He must always be stroking it. If he never loses hold of it he will be sure it is there. By way of variety, he can twist the ends. Twirling we believe, is the generally accepted term for the performance.

25 Young ladies like moustaches. Of course they do. A hero with chin whiskers or mutton-chops[3] would be nowhere. So young gentlemen, to go to our first premises – by all means raise one! Oil it. Perfume it. Comb it. Brush it. Wax it. Curl it. Twist it. Twirl it. If necessary, dye it, and on no account stop stroking it, for if you do you will show the observing world that you are thinking of something else, and what fashionable young man ever forgets the
30 existence of his moustache?

---

1 Tawny – blonde
2 Tapioca pudding – an old-fashioned rice pudding
3 Mutton-chops – a style of beard

Full reading texts

Text F   19th century

In this extract from a book on how to behave politely, the writer describes the importance of good manners when eating.

Manners

1 The style of serving dinner is different at different houses; if there are many servants they will bring you your plate filled, and you must keep it. If you have the care of a lady, see that she has what she desires, before you give your own order to the waiter; but if there are but few domestics, and the dishes are upon the table, you may with perfect propriety help
5 those near you, from any dish within your reach.

If your host or hostess passes you a plate, keep it, especially if you have chosen the food upon it, for others have also a choice, and by passing it, you may give your neighbour dishes distasteful to him, and take yourself those which he would much prefer.

I have seen men who eat soup, or chewed their food, in so noisy a manner as to be heard
10 from one end of the table to the other; fill their mouths so full of food, as to threaten suffocation or choking; use their own knife for the butter, and salt; put their fingers in the sugar bowl; and commit other faults quite as monstrous, yet seem perfectly unconscious that they were doing anything to attract attention.

Never criticize any dish before you. If a dish is distasteful to you, decline it, but make
15 no remarks about it. It is sickening and disgusting to explain at a table how one article makes you sick, or why some other dish has become distasteful to you. I have seen a well-dressed tempting dish go from a table untouched, because one of the company told a most disgusting anecdote about finding vermin[1] served in a similar dish. No wit in the narration can excuse so palpably an error of politeness.

20 Never use your knife for any purpose but to *cut* your food. It is not meant to be put in your mouth. Your fork is intended to carry the food from your plate to your mouth, and no gentleman ever eats with his knife.

It may seem a very simple thing to eat your meals, yet there is no occasion upon which the gentleman, and the low-bred, vulgar man are more strongly contrasted, than when at
25 the table.

---

1 Vermin – small animals thought to carry diseases, such as rats

Full reading texts

Text G 20th century

In this extract from a novel, the narrator describes his life in a factory, where he works on a noisy metalwork machine that makes parts for bicycles.

Saturday Night and Sunday Morning

1   Once in the shop[1] he allowed himself to be swallowed by its diverse noises, walked along lanes of capstan lathes[2] and millers, drills and polishers and hand-presses[3], worked by a multiplicity of belts and pulleys turning and twisting and slapping on heavy well-oiled wheels overhead, dependent for power on a motor stooping at the far end of the hall like
5   the black shining bulk of a stranded whale. Machines with their own small motors started with a jerk and a whine under the shadows of their operators, increasing a noise that made the brain reel and ache because the weekend had been too tranquil by contrast, a weekend that had terminated for Arthur in fishing for trout in the cool shade of a willow-sleeved canal near the Balloon Houses, miles away from the city. Motor-trolleys moved
10 up and down the main gangways carrying boxes of work – pedals, hubs, nuts, and bolts – from one part of the shop to another. Robboe the foreman bent over a stack of new timesheets behind his glass partition; women and girls wearing turbans and hair-nets and men and boys in clean blue overalls, settled down to their work, eager to get a good start on their day's stint; while sweepers and cleaners at everybody's beck and call already
15 patrolled the gangways and looked busy.

Arthur reached his capstan lathe and took off his jacket, handing it on a nearby nail so that he could keep an eye on his belongings. He pressed the starter button, and his motor came to life with a gentle thump. […] He smiled to himself and picked up a glittering steel cylinder from the top box of a pile beside him, and fixed it into the spindle. […] Monday
20 morning had lost its terror.

[…] if you went all out […] in the morning you could dawdle through the afternoon and lark about with […] your mates now and again. Such leisure often brought him near to trouble, for some weeks ago he stunned a mouse – that the overfed factory cat had missed – and laid it beneath a woman's drill, and Robboe the gaffer[4] ran out of his office when he heard
25 her screaming blue-murder, thinking that some […] woman had gone and got her hair caught in a belt[5] (big notices said that women must wear hair-nets […]) and Robboe was glad that it was nothing more than a dead mouse she was kicking up such a fuss about.

1   Shop – informal word for factory
2   Capstan lathe – machinery used to work with metal
3   millers, drills and polishers and hand-presses – machinery used to make bicycles
4   Gaffer – informal word for the manager
5   Belt – moving part of the machinery

Full reading texts

Text H   21st century

In this extract from a memoir about teaching in New York, the writer describes his first job before he started teaching, when he worked on the docks loading and unloading the cargo from ships.

Teacher Man

1   After college I passed the exams for the teacher's license but I didn't think I was cut out for the life of a teacher. I knew nothing about American teenagers. Wouldn't know what to say to you. Dockside work was easier. Trucks backed in. We swung our hooks. Haul, hoist, pull, push. Stack on pallets. Forklift slides in, lifts the load, reverses, stacks the load in the
5   warehouse, and back to the platform. You worked with your body and your brain had a day off. You worked eight to noon, had a foot-long sandwich and a quart of beer for lunch, sweated if off from one to five, headed home, hungry for dinner, ready for a movie and a few beers in a Third Avenue bar.

    Once you go the hand of it you moved like a robot. You kept up with the strongest man on
10 the platform and size didn't matter. You used your knees to save your back. If you forgot, platform men would bark, […] you got a rubber spine or sumpin'¹? You learned to use the hook different ways with different loads: boxes, sacks, crates, furniture, great chunks of greasy machinery. A sack of beans or peppers has a mind of its own. It can change shape one way or another and you have to go with it. You looked at the size, shape and weight of
15 an item and you knew in a second how to lift and swing it. You learned the ways of truckers and their helpers. Independent truckers were easy. They worked for themselves, set their own pace. Corporation² truckers prodded you to hurry up, man, lift the […] load, let's go, I wanna get outa heah³. Truckers' helpers were surly no matter who they worked for. They played little games to test you and throw you off, […]. If you worked close to the edge of
20 pier or platform they'd suddenly drop their side of the sack or crate hard enough to pull an arm from its socket and you learned to stay away from the edge of anything. Then they' laugh […]. You'd never complain to a boss about any of this. He'd say Whassa matter, kid? Can't you take a little joke? Complaining only made matters worse. The word might get to a trucker or a helper and he might accidentally bump you off the platform or even the pier. A
25 big new man […] took offense when someone put a rat's tail in his sandwich and when he threatened to kill whoever did it he was accidentally toppled into the Hudson⁴ and everyone laughed before they threw him a line and hauled him out dripping with river scum. He learned to laugh and they stopped bothering him. You can't work the piers with a long face.

---

1 Sumpin' – New York dialect for 'something'
2 Corporation – council
3 Heah – New York dialect for 'here'
4 Hudson – The Hudson River

Full reading texts

Text I   20th century

In this extract from a memoir, the writer remembers her teenage years and describes visiting the home of a much wealthier friend for tea.

Once in a House on Fire

1 'Kiwi fruit,' Tamsyn's mother announced. I was trying not to stare at the cheesecake resting on a silver stand in the middle of the table. Fleshy green coins glistened around its edge.

'It's delicious, Mrs Lee.' Wielding a spoon and fork, I acted as if I had eaten cheesecake
5 plenty of times, never mind kiwi fruit.

Tamsyn's mother and father had invited me to their house in Didsbury for tea, which they called dinner. It had been a torment to get through my lamb chop and peas without spilling. The tablecloth was white lace. Every crunch and gulp resounded in my head; no chatter cluttered the table. Tamsyn's parents spoke one at a time, in low, luxuriously slow
10 voices. In a corner of the room lurked the television, its screen a black hole. In our house, Coronation Street would be booming out while knives and forks scraped and everyone chunnered a-mile-a-minute.

'So, Andrea, what does your father do for a living?' Mr Lee leaned forward over the coffee, brewed in a glass pot after a screech of beans in the kitchen.

15 Mrs Lee darted a look at Tamsyn, then cleared her throat: 'Milk or cream?'

I glanced at Mrs Lee, wondering what Tamsyn had told her. It was a good job I hadn't blabbed more about my family. I looked down into my coffee cup as she poured in real cream.

'My dad' – I watched it swirling under the silver spoon in my cup – 'is a builder.'

20 Before Mr Lee could say anything else, Mrs Lee asked him in a tight voice: 'Are you playing golf this weekend, dear? The talk swerved to caddies and tee-times[1] and damned awkward holes.

Upstairs, in her room, Tamsyn had a desk of her own, facing a huge bay window. She let me swivel in her fancy chair while she lay on her bed, sighing about boys, wondering
25 which one on her list would turn out to be the better investment. Timothy had bought her a stuffed hippo, which she hugged under her chin while she talked.

'But then, Martin lets me read my poetry to him.' She fingered the ear of the hippo.

'You mean, you actually read your poems to other people?' The idea made me shudder. I wrote poems and stories, but I kept them pressed under a flap of carpet beneath
30 my bed.

'Course I do.' Tamsyn sat up and fiddled with her hair, admiring herself in the mirror on the door of her built-in wardrobes. 'What's the point of writing them, otherwise?'

---

1 caddies and tee-times – things related to golf

Full reading texts

Text J   21st century

In this extract from a novel about teenagers, the narrator is describing the difficulties she has living in a dangerous neighbourhood but going to school somewhere safer where the students are better off.

The Hate U Give

1   I wanna stay home and watch The Fresh Prince of Bel-Air[1], my favorite show ever, hands down. I think I know every episode word for word. Yeah it's hilarious, but it's also like seeing parts of my life on screen. I even relate to the theme song. A couple of gang members who were up to no good made trouble in my neighborhood and killed Natasha.

5   My parents got scared, and although they didn't send me to my aunt and uncle in a rich neighborhood, they sent me to a bougie[2] private school.

I just wish I could be myself at Williamson like Will was himself in Bel-Air.

I kinda wanna stay home so I can return Chris's calls too. After last night, it feels stupid to be mad at him. Or I could call Hailey and Maya, those girls Kenya claims don't count
10 as my friends. I guess I can see why she says that. I never invite them over. Why would I? They live in mini-mansions. My house is just mini.

I made the mistake of inviting them to a sleepover in seventh grade. Momma was gonna let us do our nails, stay up all night, and eat as much pizza as we wanted. It was gonna be as awesome as those weekends we had at Hailey's. The ones we still have sometimes.
15 I invited Kenya too, so I could finally hang out with all three of them at once.

Hailey didn't come. Her dad didn't want her spending the night in 'the ghetto'. I overheard my parents say that. Maya came but ended up asking her parents to come get her that night. There was a drive-by around the corner, and the gunshots scared her.

That's when I realized Williamson is one world and Garden Heights is another, and I have
20 to keep them separate.

---

1   The Fresh Prince of Bel-Air – an American TV comedy from the **1990**'s starring Will Smith
2   Bougie – luxurious or wealthy

Full reading texts

Text K   21st century

In this extract from a memoir, the musician Viv Albertine remembers meeting Colin and Raymond, two rebel boys who were allowed back in school by the headmaster after being suspended.

Clothes, clothes, clothes, music, music, music, boys, boys, boys

1   Colin and Raymond scowl up at him; they are not happy to be here or grateful for their second chance. They look at us clean-haired, well-behaved children in our maroon blazers, starched white shirts and striped ties with contempt. Their holey grey socks were crumpled around their ankles, they don't wear silly short-shorts like all the other
5   boys in my class – their shorts are long, right down to their scabby knees. They have greasy brown fringes hanging in their eyes. One of them has a scar on his freckled cheek. I think to myself, Thank goodness, two good-looking boys at school at last. I want to clap my hands together with glee. I don't know where this thought comes from. I don't recognise it. I've never cared about boys before, up until now they've been invisible to
10 me, not important in my world. […] I work all this out by myself, today – at eight years old, in Class Three.

As our class marches in a crocodile through the leafy street of Muswell Hill to the dining hall, I can't take my eyes off these two delinquents. I want to drink them in. I screw my neck round and end up walking backwards just to stare at them. I'm disappointed that
15 we're not at the same table at lunch, but at least I'm directly behind Colin, sitting at a long trestle table with my back to him. I feel excited, a new kind of excitement, a bubbling, choking, gurgling feeling rises up […] into my chest. The effort of keeping this energy contained is revving me up even more. There's only one thing I can think of doing to release the tension and get Colin's attention: I poke him in the back. He takes no notice,
20 so I poke him again. This time, he spins round and snarls at me, baring his teeth like an animal under attack, but I'm buzzing on this new feeling and once he's turned away from me, I poke him again.

'If you do that again, I'll smash your face in!'

I've never been threatened by a boy before and I don't like it, I think I might cry. I have
25 a feeling that this is not how it's supposed to go if you like someone, but the adrenalin coursing through my blood obliterates my common sense. I can't believe what I'm doing, I must be out of my mind, I risk everything, pushing all feelings of fear, pride and self-protection aside – I stretch out my arm and poke him again.

Colin swivels round. Everyone stops chattering and stares at us. I look for a teacher to
30 come and save me but nobody's near so I grip the bench tightly and stare straight back at Colin, waiting for the punch. His mouth twists into a sly smile.

'I think she likes me.'

From this moment on, we are inseparable.

103

Full reading texts

Text L   20th century

In this extract from a novel, a young boy called Marcus describes how he feels different to the other students at his school.

About a Boy

1 He got to school early, went to the form room, sat down at his desk. He was safe enough there. The kids who had given him a hard time yesterday were probably not the sort to arrive at school first thing; they'd be off somewhere smoking […] he thought darkly. There were a couple of girls in the room, but they ignored him, unless the snort of laughter he
5 heard while he was getting his reading book out had anything to do with him.

What was there to laugh at? Not much, really, unless you were the kind of person who was on permanent lookout for something to laugh at. Unfortunately, that was exactly the kind of person most kids were, in his experience. They patrolled up and down school corridors like sharks, except that what they were on the lookout for wasn't flesh but the
10 wrong trousers, or the wrong haircut, or the wrong shoes, any or all of which sent them wild with excitement. As he was usually wearing the wrong shoes or the wrong trousers, and his haircut was wrong all the time, every day of the week, he didn't have to do very much to send them demented.

Marcus knew he was weird, and he knew that part of the reason he was weird was
15 because his mum was weird. She just didn't get this, any of it. She was always telling him that only shallow people made judgements on the basis of clothes or hair she didn't want him to watch rubbish television, or listen to rubbish music, or play rubbish computer games (she thought they were all rubbish) which meant that if he wanted to do anything that any of the other kids spent their time doing he had to argue with her for hours. He
20 usually lost, and she was so good at arguing that he felt good about losing. She could explain why listening to Joni Mitchell[1] and Bob Marley[2] [who happened to be her two favourite singers] was much better for him that listening to Snoop Doggy Dogg and why it was more important to read books than to play on the Gameboy his dad had given him. But he couldn't pass any of this on to the kids at school. If he tried to tell Lee Hartley – the
25 biggest and loudest and nastiest of the kids he'd met yesterday – that he didn't approve of Snoop Doggy Dogg because Snoop Doggy Dogg had a bad attitude to women Lee Hartley would thump him, or call him something that he didn't want to be called.

---

1 Joni Mitchell – a famous female singer from the **1960s**
2 Bob Marley – a famous reggae singer from the **1970s**